SOUP RECIPES

100 Simple and Delicious Soup Recipes for a Healthy Life

INNA VOLIA

TABLE OF CONTENTS

INTRODUCTION 6
Health Benefits of Soup 7
Helpful Tips for Soup Making 8
Tips for Soup Makers 9
1-Healthy Tomato Carrot Soup 10
2-Curried Carrot Soup 12
3-Classic Squash Soup 14
4-Lemon Thyme Asparagus Soup 16
5-Ginger Carrot Soup 18
6-Tasty Chicken Noodle Soup 20
7-Healthy Salad Soup 22
8-Simple Potato Leek Soup 24
9-Creamy Chicken Soup 26
10-Chili Squash Soup 28
11-Asian Chicken Corn Soup 30
12-Yummy Chicken Noodle Soup 32
13-Tarragon Chicken Soup 34
14-Spicy Tomato Pepper Soup 36
15-Delicious Apple Parsnip Soup 38
16-Green Lentil Sausage Soup 40
17-Sweet Beetroot Soup 42
18-Cheese Cauliflower Soup 44
19-Roasted Carrot Soup 46
20-Lentil Paprika Soup 48
21-Cheese Broccoli Soup 50
22-Chicken Tortilla Soup 52
23-Peanut Butter Carrot Soup 54
24- Chicken Vegetable Soup 56
25-Tasty Chicken Noodle Soup 58

26-Spicy Mushroom Soup 60
27-Beef Kale Soup 62
28-Pumpkin Spice Cauliflower Soup 64
29-Chicken Kale Soup 66
30-Coconut Potato Soup 68
31-Garlic Squash Cauliflower Soup 70
32-Thyme Nutmeg Squash Soup 72
33-Yummy Tomato Basil Soup 74
34-Cabbage Tomato Soup 76
35-Asparagus Bacon Soup 78
36-Celery Coconut Soup 80
37-Spinach Broccoli Soup 82
38-Pumpkin Coconut Soup 84
39-Easy Zucchini Soup 86
40-Coconut Curried Carrot Soup 88
41-Celery Chicken Soup 90
42-Italian Cabbage Soup 92
43-Creamy Broccoli Carrot Soup 94
44-Chicken Spinach Mushroom Soup 96
45-Onion Soup 98
46-Sweet Potato Bean Soup 100
47-Kale Potato Soup 102
48-Salsa Corn Bean Soup 104
49-Pea Carrot Soup 106
50-Potato Carrot Soup 108
51-White Bean Carrot Soup 110
52-Healthy Red Lentil Carrot Soup 112
53-Cabbage Pork Soup 114
54-Turmeric Tomato Soup 116
55-Chicken Tomato Soup 118
56-Zesty Tomato Cabbage Soup 120

57-Chickpea Tomato Soup 122
58-Healthy Vegetable Soup.. 124
59-Simple & Yummy Chicken Soup 126
60-Creamy Vegetable Soup.. 128
61-Creamy Basil Zucchini Soup 130
62- Delicious Onion Soup 132
63-Brussels Sprout Soup..134
64-Tomato Chickpea Soup...136
65-Eastern Lentil Soup 138
66-Avocado Soup 140
67-Tomato White Bean Soup 142
68-Apple Sweet Potato Soup... 144
69-Cinnamon Apple Squash Soup 146
70-Italian Chicken Soup... 148
71-Simple Asparagus Soup 150
72-Mushroom Cauliflower Soup...152
73-Cinnamon Broccoli Avocado Soup 154
74-Cauliflower Leek Soup 156
75-Delicious Tomato Pumpkin Soup 158
76-Flavorful Herb Tomato Soup 160
77-Kale Spinach Soup 162
78-Coconut Celery Soup... 164
79-Cauliflower Watercress Soup... 166
80-Simple Asparagus Soup.. 168
81-Brown Lentil Soup 169
82-Onion Shallot Soup... 171
83-Cheese Tomato Soup 173
84-Creamy Mushroom Soup..175
85-Cheddar Broccoli Soup 177
86-Cauliflower Roasted Pepper Soup 179
87-Green Cauliflower Soup..181

88-Curried Summer Squash Soup 183
89-Simple Potato Soup 185
90-Sausage Potato Soup 186
91-Easy Tomato Soup 188
92-Cream of Mushroom Soup 190
93-Healthy Red Lentil Soup 192
94-Turmeric Tomato Soup 194
95-Healthy Anti-inflammatory Broccoli Soup 196
96-Green Vegetable Soup 198
97-Chunky Bean Vegetable Soup...200
98-Classic Leek Potato Soup... 202
99-Sweet Corn Soup.. 204
100-Broccoli Bean Soup.. 206
CONCLUSION: 208

INTRODUCTION

Soup is a delicious and hot meal which provides several health benefits. It is made up of healthy and nutrient-rich vegetables and helps to reduce your food cravings while keeping you energized. Soups are typically low in calories, so if you are trying to lose or maintain your body weight, soup is the best option in your daily diet. The simplest recipes require few ingredients and are easy to make, so you can easily enjoy it at any time.

Vegetable soup contains many vitamins, such as vitamin A, vitamin C, vitamin D, and calcium. Studies prove that tomato soup is the best source of antioxidants and lycopene which can help reduce the risk of cancer. Soups made up of meat, fish and beans contain lean protein and fiber. The healthiest soup includes fresh vegetables, low-fat ingredients and a minimal amount of salt. Soup isn't just for the cold seasons, you can consume soup even in the summer!

Health Benefits of Soup:

- Soup is considered to be a highly nutritious meal as it is made up of a combination of different ingredients including fresh vegetables, fruits, grains, herbs, meats, and spices.
- Soup works as an energy booster; it contains proteins, carbohydrates, and various nutrients. Soup is also easy to digest and provides a steady supply of energy to our body.
- Soup is easy to prepare and is also economical as it simply requires some fresh vegetables and few overall the ingredients.
- Soup helps to reduce or maintain your body weight because it contains minimal calories while being rich in nutrients.
- Research proves that miso and other soy-based soups help lower your risk of breast cancer.
- Soups provide various vitamins like vitamins A, C, and D, as well as calcium and fiber. Lentil soup is especially rich in fibers - it contains 4-5 grams of fiber per serving.

Helpful Tips for Soup Making:

- Use aromatics such as celery, onion, leeks, carrots, and garlic. Sauté these aromatics in a pan over medium heat before adding the other ingredients to bring out their flavor.
- Always use a good base. Broth and stocks can be made at home or bought pre-made. Always use hot stocks when making soup.
- Use the right tools. For example, if you want to make a large quantity of soup, use a heavy stock pot, a good soup ladle, food processor or a blender.
- Season your soups. You can use a dollop of sour cream, a sprinkle of fresh herbs, a squeeze of citrus, etc.
- Garnish your soup before serving it. You can use fresh herbs for rich broths, crushed croutons for creamy soups, bacon for sweet soups, sour cream for chunky soups, etc.

Tips for Soup Makers:

- Get all your ingredients ready before making your soup.
- Add only boneless meat to the soup maker.
- Chop your ingredients into small pieces before adding them to the soup maker.
- Always use hot stock or hot water.
- Make sure the soup maker's lid is tightly sealed and fastened before cooking.
- Follow the manufacturer's instructions when using the appliance.
- Do not overfill your soup maker. Pay careful attention to the capacity of your soup maker and the fill level markers.

1-Healthy Tomato Carrot Soup

Time: 35 minutes

Serve: 2

Ingredients:

- 3 large tomatoes, chopped
- 6 medium carrots, peeled and chopped
- 1 onion, peeled and chopped
- 2 red bell peppers, diced
- ½ tsp cayenne pepper
- ¾ tsp chili powder
- 2 vegetable cubes
- 1 tsp garlic paste
- 2 cans of tomatoes
- 3.5 oz butternut squash, peeled and cubed
- 1 leek, chopped
- 1 cup of water
- Pepper
- Salt

Directions:

- Add all the ingredients into the soup maker and stir well.
- Select the chunky mode on the soup maker and set the timer for 28 minutes.
- Season the soup with salt and pepper.
- Serve and enjoy.

Nutritional Value (Amount per Serving):

- Calories 282
- Fat 2 g
- Carbohydrates 64.6 g
- Sugar 27.5 g
- Protein 9.2 g
- Cholesterol 0 mg

2-Curried Carrot Soup

Time: 30 minutes

Serve: 4

Ingredients:

- ¾ lb carrot, peeled and cut into chunks
- ½ cup of coconut milk
- 2 tsp curry powder
- 3 cups of vegetable stock
- 1 onion, chopped
- 1 potato, peeled and chopped
- Pepper
- Salt

Directions:

- Add all the ingredients except coconut milk into the soup maker.
- Close the soup maker's lid and cook on smooth mode for 23 minutes.
- Add coconut milk and stir well.
- Serve and enjoy.

Nutritional Value (Amount per Serving):

- Calories 151
- Fat 7.9 g
- Carbohydrates 21.1 g
- Sugar 7.2 g
- Protein 2.7 g
- Cholesterol 0 mg

3-Classic Squash Soup

Time: 31 minutes

Serve: 4

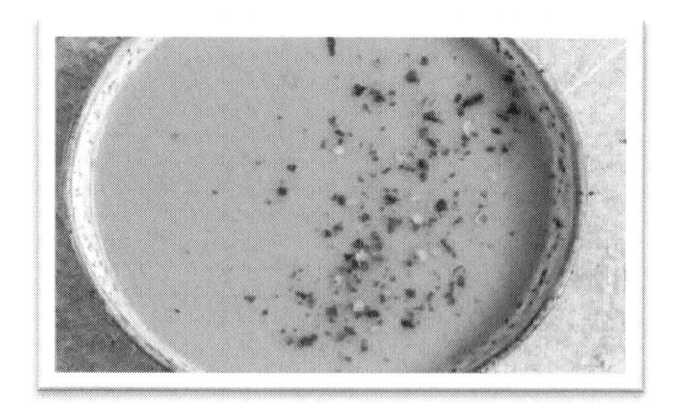

Ingredients:

- 1 butternut squash, peeled and chopped
- 3 ¼ cups of vegetable stock
- 2 medium potatoes, peeled and chopped
- 2 garlic cloves, crushed
- 1 onion, chopped
- 1 tbsp olive oil
- Pepper
- Salt

Directions:

- Heat the oil in a pan over medium heat.
- Add the garlic and onion to the pan and sauté until the onion softens.
- Transfer the sautéed onion and garlic to the soup maker along with the remaining ingredients.

- Seal the soup maker with its lid and cook on smooth mode for 21 minutes.
- Season soup with salt and pepper.
- Serve and enjoy.

Nutritional Value (Amount per Serving):

- Calories 135
- Fat 4.2 g
- Carbohydrates 24.4 g
- Sugar 3.7 g
- Protein 2.5 g
- Cholesterol 0 mg

4-Lemon Thyme Asparagus Soup

Time: 35 minutes

Serve: 4

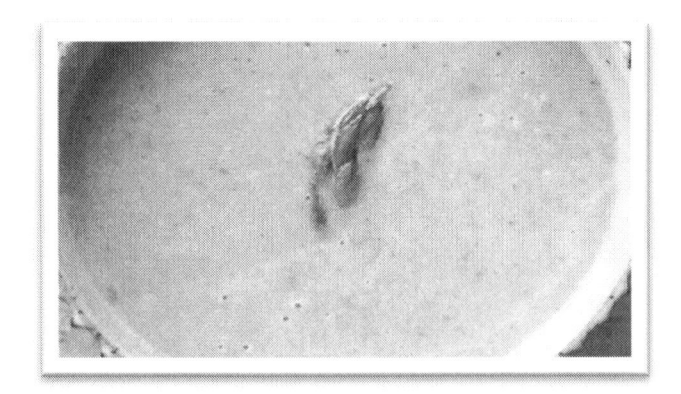

Ingredients:

- 1 lb asparagus, woody ends removed, sliced
- 3 chicken stock cubes
- ½ tsp thyme
- 1 tbsp fresh lemon juice
- 1 leek, sliced
- 2 garlic cloves, minced
- 1 onion, diced
- 3 ¼ cups of water
- 1 tbsp olive oil
- Pepper
- Salt

Directions:

- Heat oil in a pan over medium heat.
- Add asparagus, thyme, leek, garlic, and onion to the pan and sauté over medium-low heat for 10 minutes.

- Transfer sautéed vegetable mixture to the soup maker along with remaining ingredients.
- Seal the soup maker with its lid and cook on smooth mode for 21 minutes.
- Season soup with salt and pepper.
- Serve and enjoy.

Nutritional Value (Amount per Serving):

- Calories 88
- Fat 4 g
- Carbohydrates 11.7 g
- Sugar 4.3 g
- Protein 3.8 g
- Cholesterol 0 mg

5-Ginger Carrot Soup

Time: 35 minutes

Serve: 2

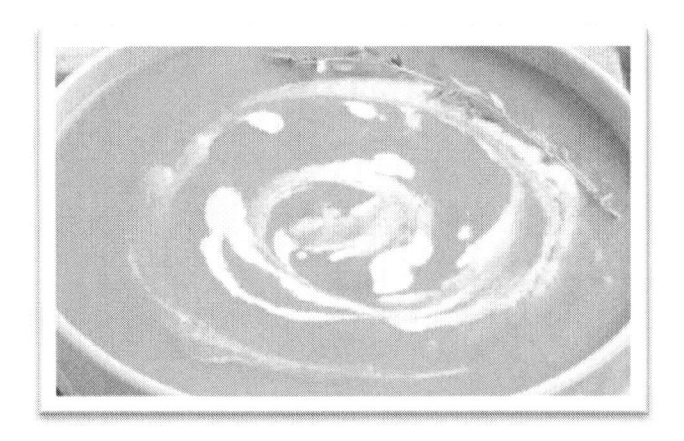

Ingredients:

- 12 carrots, peeled and chopped
- 4 tbsp yogurt
- 2 ½ cups of water
- 1 tsp oregano
- 1 tbsp ginger, peeled and chopped
- 2 spring onion, diced
- Pepper
- Salt

Directions:

- Add all the ingredients except yogurt into the soup maker.
- Seal the soup maker with its lid and cook for 25 minutes on the cook and blend mode.
- Add yogurt and stir well.

- Season with salt and pepper.
- Serve and enjoy.

Nutritional Value (Amount per Serving):

- Calories 188
- Fat 0.6 g
- Carbohydrates 41.7 g
- Sugar 20.6 g
- Protein 5.4 g
- Cholesterol 2 mg

6-Tasty Chicken Noodle Soup

Time: 35 minutes

Serve: 4

Ingredients:

- 1 chicken breast, cut into bite-size pieces
- ½ cup of water
- 2 tbsp butter
- 2 tsp paprika
- ¾ tsp thyme
- 1 ½ tsp tarragon
- 1 ½ tsp basil
- 1 ½ tsp oregano
- 1 onion, chopped
- 1 carrot, peeled and diced
- 5.3 oz linguine
- Pepper
- Salt

Directions:

- Add all the ingredients except butter into the soup maker.
- Seal the soup maker with its lid and cook on chunky mode for 25 minutes.
- Add butter and stir well.
- Season with salt and pepper.
- Serve and enjoy.

Nutritional Value (Amount per Serving):

- Calories 214
- Fat 7.6 g
- Carbohydrates 25.9 g
- Sugar 2.1 g
- Protein 11 g
- Cholesterol 61 mg

7-Healthy Salad Soup

Time: 35 minutes

Serve: 4

Ingredients:

- 1/3 cabbage, chopped
- 1 ½ tsp oregano
- ½ cup of water
- 2 tomatoes, chopped
- 2 celery sticks, chopped
- 4 carrots, peeled and chopped
- 1 red bell pepper, diced
- 1 green bell pepper, diced
- Pepper
- Salt

Directions:

- Add all the ingredients to the soup maker.
- Seal the soup maker with its lid and cook for 25 minutes on cook and blend mode.
- Season soup with salt and pepper.

- Serve and enjoy.

Nutritional Value (Amount per Serving):

- Calories 74
- Fat 0.4 g
- Carbohydrates 17 g
- Sugar 9.4 g
- Protein 2.7 g
- Cholesterol 0 mg

8-Simple Potato Leek Soup

Time: 31 minutes

Serve: 4

Ingredients:

- 1 lb potatoes, peeled and chopped
- 1 vegetable stock cube
- 3 cups of hot water
- ½ cup fresh cream
- 1 onion, chopped
- 1 cup leek, chopped
- Pepper
- Salt

Directions:

- Add all the ingredients to the soup maker and stir well.
- Seal the soup maker with its lid and cook on smooth mode for 21 minutes.
- Season soup with salt and pepper.
- Serve and enjoy.

Nutritional Value (Amount per Serving):

- Calories 125
- Fat 2 g
- Carbohydrates 24.8 g
- Sugar 3.9 g
- Protein 2.9 g
- Cholesterol 6 mg

9-Creamy Chicken Soup

Time: 31 minutes

Serve: 3

Ingredients:

- ½ lb chicken, cut into small pieces
- 2 ½ cup water
- 2 chicken stock cubes
- 1 tsp thyme
- ¾ cup milk
- 2 celery stalk, chopped
- 1 carrot, peeled and chopped
- 2 leeks, sliced
- 1 onion, diced
- 2 potatoes, peeled and diced
- Pepper
- Salt

Directions:

- Spray pan with cooking spray and heat over medium heat.
- Add chicken and onion to the pan and sauté until onion is translucent.
- Add all the vegetables and thyme and cook for 10 minutes.
- Transfer the pan mixture to the soup maker along with the remaining ingredients.
- Seal the soup maker with its lid and cook on smooth mode for 21 minutes.
- Season soup with salt and pepper.
- Serve and enjoy.

Nutritional Value (Amount per Serving):

- Calories 311
- Fat 4.1 g
- Carbohydrates 40.5 g
- Sugar 9.4 g
- Protein 28.3 g
- Cholesterol 64 mg

10-Chili Squash Soup

Time: 50 minutes

Serve: 4

Ingredients:

- 1 large butternut squash, cut into chunks
- 3 garlic cloves, peeled
- 3 cups of vegetable stock
- 1 potato, peeled and cut into chunks
- 1 onion, chopped
- 1 red chili, chopped
- Pepper
- Salt

Directions:

- Preheat the oven to 200 C/ 400 F.
- Place squash, chili, garlic, and potato on baking tray and roast in preheated oven for 20 minutes.
- Add roasted vegetables to the soup maker along with remaining ingredients.

- Seal the soup maker with its lid and cook on smooth mode for 21 minutes.
- Season soup with salt and pepper.
- Serve and enjoy.

Nutritional Value (Amount per Serving):

- Calories 63
- Fat 1.7 g
- Carbohydrates 13.9 g
- Sugar 4.1 g
- Protein 1.9 g
- Cholesterol 0 mg

11-Asian Chicken Corn Soup

Time: 40 minutes

Serve: 4

Ingredients:

- ½ lb chicken, cooked and shredded
- 2 tbsp fresh coriander, chopped
- 1 red chili, chopped
- 2 spring onion, chopped
- 2 tsp cornflour, stir with 1 tsp of water
- 3 ¼ cup chicken stock
- 1 tsp ginger, grated
- 3.5 oz water chestnuts, sliced
- 1 onion, chopped
- 11 oz sweet corn
- Pepper
- Salt

Directions:

- Add all the ingredients to the soup maker.
- Seal the soup maker with its lid and cook for 30 minutes on chunky mode.
- Season soup with salt and pepper.
- Serve hot and enjoy.

Nutritional Value (Amount per Serving):

- Calories 514
- Fat 7.4 g
- Carbohydrates 93.4 g
- Sugar 15.7 g
- Protein 31.9 g
- Cholesterol 44 mg

12-Yummy Chicken Noodle Soup

Time: 38 minutes

Serve: 4

Ingredients:

- ½ lb chicken, cooked and shredded
- 4 cups of water
- 1 tbsp flour
- ½ lb potatoes, peeled and cubed
- 1 chicken stock cube
- 3 oz chicken noodles
- Pepper
- Salt

Directions:

- Add all the ingredients to the soup maker.
- Cover soup maker with lid and cook on chunky mode for 28 minutes.
- Season soup with salt and pepper.
- Serve and enjoy.

Nutritional Value (Amount per Serving):

- Calories 140
- Fat 2.1 g
- Carbohydrates 11.3 g
- Sugar 0.7 g
- Protein 18 g
- Cholesterol 45 mg

13-Tarragon Chicken Soup

Time: 31 minutes

Serve: 2

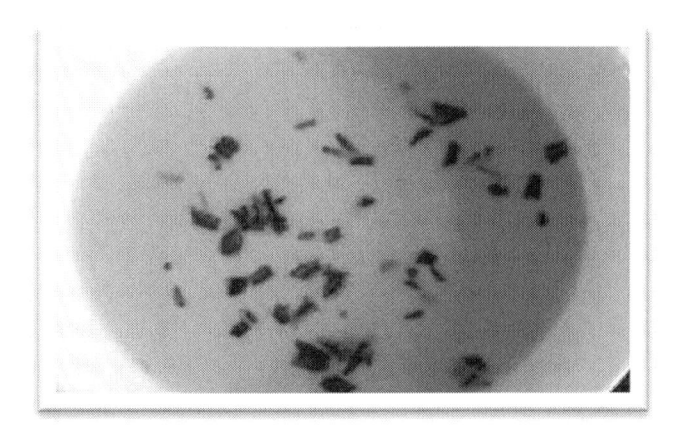

Ingredients:

- 5.2 oz chicken, cooked and shredded
- 1 tbsp olive oil
- 2 garlic cloves, chopped
- 1 onion, chopped
- 2/3 cup cream
- 2 tbsp fresh tarragon, chopped
- 1 chicken stock cube

Directions:

- Add all the ingredients to the soup maker and stir well.
- Fill soup maker up to the minimum line with boiling water.
- Cover soup maker with lid and cook on smooth mode for 21 minutes.
- Season soup with salt and pepper.

- Serve warm and enjoy.

Nutritional Value (Amount per Serving):

- Calories 259
- Fat 14 g
- Carbohydrates 10.1 g
- Sugar 4 g
- Protein 23.6 g
- Cholesterol 72 mg

14-Spicy Tomato Pepper Soup

Time: 51 minutes

Serve: 4

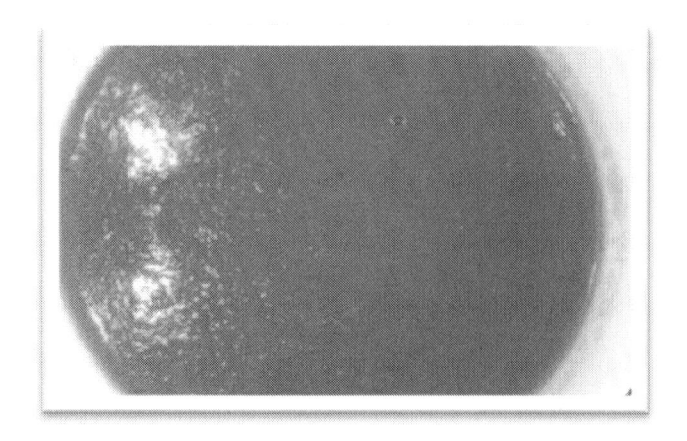

Ingredients:

- 1 lb fresh tomatoes, halved
- 2 peppers, sliced
- 1 tbsp olive oil
- 2 tsp chili flakes
- 3 garlic cloves, chopped
- 2 cups of vegetable stock
- 14 oz can tomatoes
- 1 onion, sliced
- Pepper
- Salt

Directions:

- Preheat the oven to 200 C/ 400 F.
- Place tomatoes and peppers on baking tray and drizzle with olive oil.

- Roast tomatoes and peppers in preheated oven for 20 minutes.
- Transfer roasted tomatoes and peppers to the soup maker along with remaining ingredients.
- Seal the soup maker with its lid and cook on smooth mode for 21 minutes.
- Season soup with salt and pepper.
- Serve and enjoy.

Nutritional Value (Amount per Serving):

- Calories 91
- Fat 4.8 g
- Carbohydrates 13.9 g
- Sugar 8.6 g
- Protein 2.4 g
- Cholesterol 0 mg

15-Delicious Apple Parsnip Soup

Time: 41 minutes

Serve: 6

Ingredients:

- 1 lb apples, peeled and chopped
- 1 lb parsnips, cut into chunks
- 5 oz milk
- 4 cups of vegetable stock
- 2 garlic cloves, chopped
- 1 large onion, chopped
- 1 tbsp olive oil
- 1 oz butter
- Pepper
- Salt

Directions:

- Heat butter and oil in a pan over medium heat.
- Add onion and parsnips to the pan and sauté until onion softens about 10 minutes.

- Transfer sautéed onion and parsnips to the soup maker along with remaining ingredients.
- Seal the soup maker with its lid and cook on smooth mode for 21 minutes.
- Season soup with salt and pepper.
- Serve and enjoy.

Nutritional Value (Amount per Serving):

- Calories 160
- Fat 8.3 g
- Carbohydrates 23.9 g
- Sugar 11 g
- Protein 2.2 g
- Cholesterol 12 mg

16-Green Lentil Sausage Soup

Time: 43 minutes

Serve: 4

Ingredients:

- ¼ cup green lentils, rinsed and drained
- 1 tsp olive oil
- 2 tbsp fresh parsley, chopped
- 2.5 oz sausage, cubed
- 1 onion, diced
- 1 large carrot, peeled and chopped
- 2 potatoes, peeled and cubed
- 5 ¼ cups of chicken stock
- Pepper
- Salt

Directions:

- Heat oil in a pan over medium heat.
- Add onion to the pan and sauté for 5 minutes.

- Transfer sautéed onion to the soup maker along with remaining ingredients.
- Seal the soup maker with its lid and cook on chunky mode for 28 minutes.
- Season soup with salt and pepper.
- Serve and enjoy.

Nutritional Value (Amount per Serving):

- Calories 218
- Fat 7.2 g
- Carbohydrates 29.4 g
- Sugar 4.5 g
- Protein 9.7 g
- Cholesterol 15 mg

17-Sweet Beetroot Soup

Time: 38 minutes

Serve: 6

Ingredients:

- 5 medium beetroots, peeled and cubed
- ¼ cup fresh cream
- 1 tbsp sugar
- 6 ½ cup vegetable stock
- 2 carrots, peeled and sliced
- Pepper
- Salt

Directions:

- Add all the ingredients except cream into the soup maker.
- Seal the soup maker with its lid and cook on chunky mode for 28 minutes.
- Add cream and stir well. Season with salt and pepper.
- Serve and enjoy.

Nutritional Value (Amount per Serving):

- Calories 61
- Fat 1 g
- Carbohydrates 13 g
- Sugar 10.2 g
- Protein 1.7 g
- Cholesterol 2 mg

18-Cheese Cauliflower Soup

Time: 38 minutes

Serve: 4

Ingredients:

- ¾ lb cauliflower, cut into florets
- 3 tbsp cheddar cheese, grated
- ½ cup cream
- 2 tbsp fresh dill, chopped
- 6 ½ cups of vegetable stock
- 2 potatoes, peeled and cubed
- 2 carrots, peeled and sliced
- Pepper
- Salt

Directions:

- Add all the ingredients except cheese and cream to the soup maker.
- Seal the soup maker with its lid and cook on chunky mode for 28 minutes.

- Add cream and cheese and stir well.
- Season with salt and pepper.
- Serve and enjoy.

Nutritional Value (Amount per Serving):

- Calories 168
- Fat 7 g
- Carbohydrates 29.4 g
- Sugar 8.6 g
- Protein 5.6 g
- Cholesterol 11 mg

19-Roasted Carrot Soup

Time: 61 minutes

Serve: 4

Ingredients:

- 7 large carrots, peeled and cubed
- 1 tbsp olive oil
- 1 sweet potato, peeled and cubed
- 1 large onion, chopped
- ½ cup fresh coriander, chopped
- 6 ½ cups of vegetable stock
- Pepper
- Salt

Directions:

- Preheat the oven to 200 C/ 400 F.
- Place sweet potato, onion, and carrot on a baking dish and drizzle with oil.
- Roast vegetables in preheated oven for 30 minutes.
- Transfer roasted veggie in soup maker along with remaining ingredients.

- Seal the soup maker with its lid and cook on smooth mode for 21 minutes.
- Season soup with salt and pepper.
- Serve and enjoy.

Nutritional Value (Amount per Serving):

- Calories 125
- Fat 4.1 g
- Carbohydrates 22.4 g
- Sugar 10.2 g
- Protein 2.1 g
- Cholesterol 0 mg

20-Lentil Paprika Soup

Time: 31 minutes

Serve: 4

Ingredients:

- 6.2 oz split red lentils
- 1 tsp olive oil
- ¾ tsp smoked paprika
- 6 cups of vegetable stock
- 14 oz can tomatoes
- 2 tsp tomato puree
- 2 garlic cloves, chopped
- 2 carrots, peeled and chopped
- 1 potato, peeled and chopped
- 1 celery stalk, chopped
- Pepper
- Salt

Directions:

- Add all the ingredients to the soup maker.
- Cover soup maker with lid and cook on smooth mode.
- Season soup with salt and pepper.
- Serve warm and enjoy.

Nutritional Value (Amount per Serving):

- Calories 252
- Fat 4.8 g
- Carbohydrates 46 g
- Sugar 9.3 g
- Protein 13.6 g
- Cholesterol 0 mg

21-Cheese Broccoli Soup

Time: 31 minutes

Serve: 4

Ingredients:

- 4 cups of broccoli florets
- ¼ cup gorgonzola cheese, crumbled
- 1 tsp thyme
- 1 potato, peeled and cubed
- 3 garlic cloves
- 6 cup vegetable stock
- Pepper
- Salt

Directions:

- Add all the ingredients to the soup maker except cheese and stir well.
- Seal the soup maker with its lid and cook on smooth mode.
- Top with crumbled cheese. Season with salt and pepper.
- Serve and enjoy.

Nutritional Value (Amount per Serving):

- Calories 120
- Fat 6.4 g
- Carbohydrates 18.1 g
- Sugar 4.9 g
- Protein 5.9 g
- Cholesterol 10 mg

22-Chicken Tortilla Soup

Time: 43 minutes

Serve: 6

Ingredients:

- 2 cups of chicken, cooked and diced
- 42 oz can chicken broth
- 7 oz can tomatoes, diced
- 7 oz can corn
- 1 tsp thyme
- 1 jalapeno pepper, chopped
- ½ onion, chopped
- 1 tbsp butter
- ½ tsp black pepper
- 1 tsp salt

Directions:

- Melt butter in a pan over medium heat.
- Add jalapeno and onion to the pan and sauté for 5 minutes.

- Transfer sautéed onion and jalapeno to the soup maker along with remaining ingredients.
- Cover soup maker with lid and cook on chunky mode.
- Garnish soup with tortilla chips and serve.

Nutritional Value (Amount per Serving):

- Calories 140
- Fat 3.7 g
- Carbohydrates 9.9 g
- Sugar 3 g
- Protein 17.6 g
- Cholesterol 41 mg

23-Peanut Butter Carrot Soup

Time: 31 minutes

Serve: 4

Ingredients:

- 8 carrots, peeled and chopped
- 1 onion, chopped
- 1 ½ cup chicken stock
- ¼ cup peanut butter
- 1 tbsp curry paste
- 3 garlic cloves, peeled
- 14 oz coconut milk
- Pepper
- Salt

Directions:

- Add all the ingredients to the soup maker.
- Cover soup maker with lid and cook on smooth mode for 21 minutes.
- Season soup with salt and pepper.
- Serve hot and enjoy.

Nutritional Value (Amount per Serving):

- Calories 416
- Fat 34.2 g
- Carbohydrates 25.3 g
- Sugar 12.3 g
- Protein 8.2 g
- Cholesterol 0 mg

24- Chicken Vegetable Soup

Time: 38 minutes

Serve: 6

Ingredients:

- 2 chicken breasts, cut into cube
- ½ tsp red pepper flakes
- ¼ cup fresh parsley, chopped
- 1 tsp garlic powder
- 3 cups of chicken broth
- 14 oz can tomatoes, diced
- ¼ cup cabbage, shredded
- 1 cup of frozen green beans
- ¼ cup frozen peas
- 3 garlic cloves, minced
- ½ onion, chopped
- ½ cup of frozen corn
- 2 celery stalk, chopped
- 1 carrot, peeled and cubed
- ½ sweet potato, peeled and cubed
- ½ tsp pepper
- 1 tsp salt

Directions:

- Add all the ingredients to the soup maker.
- Cover soup maker with lid and cook on chunky mode.
- Season soup with salt and pepper.
- Serve warm and enjoy.

Nutritional Value (Amount per Serving):

- Calories 171
- Fat 4.6 g
- Carbohydrates 13.9 g
- Sugar 5.4 g
- Protein 18.9 g
- Cholesterol 0 mg

25-Tasty Chicken Noodle Soup

Time: 38 minutes

Serve: 6

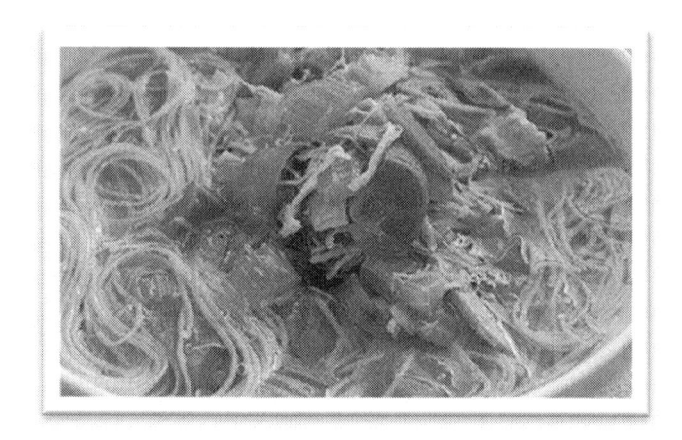

Ingredients:

- 6 cups of chicken, cooked and cubed
- 3 tbsp rice vinegar
- 2 ½ cups of cabbage, shredded
- 8 oz rice noodles
- 1 bell pepper, chopped
- 1 large carrot, peeled and sliced
- 6 cups of chicken stock
- 2 celery stalks, sliced
- 1 onion, chopped
- 2 tbsp fresh ginger, grated
- 2 tbsp soy sauce
- 3 garlic cloves, minced
- ½ tsp black pepper

Directions:

- Add all the ingredients to the soup maker.
- Cover soup maker with lid and cook on chunky mode.
- Season soup with salt and pepper.
- Serve and enjoy.

Nutritional Value (Amount per Serving):

- Calories 306
- Fat 5.1 g
- Carbohydrates 18.7 g
- Sugar 4.3 g
- Protein 43.1 g
- Cholesterol 0 mg

26-Spicy Mushroom Soup

Time: 31 minutes

Serve: 2

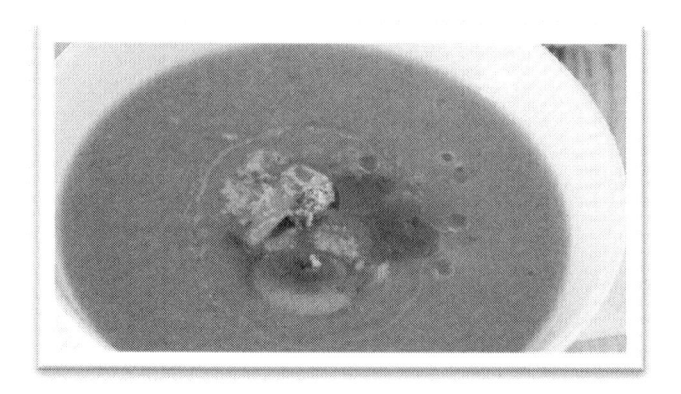

Ingredients:

- 1 cup mushrooms, chopped
- ½ tsp chili powder
- 2 tsp garam masala
- 2 garlic cloves, crushed
- 1 onion, chopped
- 3 tbsp olive oil
- 1 tsp fresh lemon juice
- 5 cups of chicken stock
- ¼ cup fresh celery, chopped
- ½ tsp black pepper
- 1 tsp sea salt

Directions:

- Heat oil in a pan over medium heat.
- Add onion and garlic to the pan and sauté for 5 minutes.

- Add garam masala and chili powder and sauté for a minute.
- Transfer sautéed onion and garlic to the soup maker.
- Add remaining ingredients and close soup maker with lid and cook on smooth mode.
- Serve and enjoy.

Nutritional Value (Amount per Serving):

- Calories 244
- Fat 22.8 g
- Carbohydrates 10.2 g
- Sugar 5 g
- Protein 3.9 g
- Cholesterol 0 mg

27-Beef Kale Soup

Time: 46 minutes

Serve: 4

Ingredients:

- 1 lb beef stew meat
- 1 tsp cayenne pepper
- 1 cup kale, chopped
- 1 onion, sliced
- 3 garlic cloves, crushed
- 4 cups of chicken broth
- 2 tbsp olive oil
- ¼ tsp black pepper
- ½ tsp salt

Directions:

- Heat oil in a pan over medium heat.
- Add onion and garlic to the pan and sauté for 3 minutes.
- Add meat to the pan and sauté for 5 minutes.

- Transfer sautéed pa mixture to the soup maker along with remaining ingredients except for kale.
- Seal the soup maker with its lid and cook on chunky mode.
- Add kale and stir well and let sit for 10 minutes.
- Serve and enjoy.

Nutritional Value (Amount per Serving):

- Calories 333
- Fat 15.6 g
- Carbohydrates 6.3 g
- Sugar 1.9 g
- Protein 40.3 g
- Cholesterol 0 mg

28-Pumpkin Spice Cauliflower Soup

Time: 36 minutes

Serve: 4

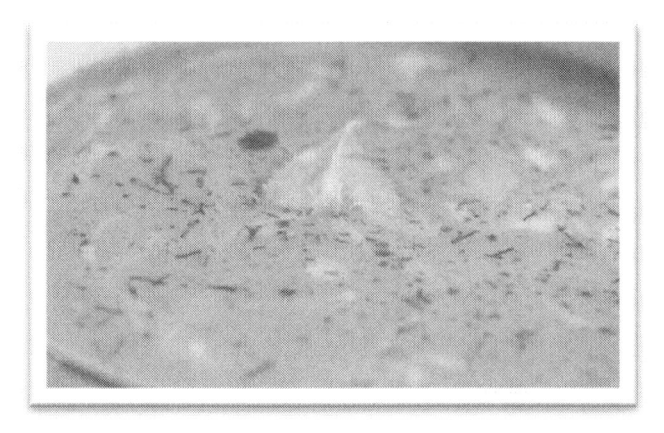

Ingredients:

- 2 cups of cauliflower florets
- 5 cups of chicken broth
- 3 tbsp olive oil
- 1 tsp pumpkin pie spice
- 1 onion, chopped
- ¼ tsp salt

Directions:

- Heat oil in a pan over medium heat.
- Add onion to the pan and sauté for 5 minutes.
- Add cauliflower and sauté for a minute.
- Transfer sautéed onion and cauliflower to the soup maker along with remaining ingredients.
- Seal the soup maker with its lid and cook on smooth mode.
- Serve and enjoy.

Nutritional Value (Amount per Serving):

- Calories 163
- Fat 12.3 g
- Carbohydrates 6.7 g
- Sugar 3.3 g
- Protein 7.4 g
- Cholesterol 0 mg

29-Chicken Kale Soup

Time: 38 minutes

Serve: 4

Ingredients:

- 2 cups of chicken breast, cooked and shredded
- 2 tsp garlic, minced
- ½ tsp cinnamon
- 4 cups of chicken stock
- 1 onion, diced
- 12 oz kale
- 1 tsp salt

Directions:

- Add all the ingredients to the soup maker.
- Cover soup maker with lid and cook on chunky mode.
- Season soup with salt and pepper.
- Serve and enjoy.

Nutritional Value (Amount per Serving):

- Calories 158
- Fat 2.8 g
- Carbohydrates 13.1 g
- Sugar 1 g
- Protein 19.7 g
- Cholesterol 0 mg

30-Coconut Potato Soup

Time: 25 minutes

Serve: 6

Ingredients:

- 3 lbs russet potatoes, peeled and diced
- 15 oz can coconut milk
- 3 garlic cloves, minced
- 1 onion, chopped
- 2 tbsp olive oil
- 3 cups of chicken broth
- ½ tsp dried thyme
- 2 carrots, peeled and sliced
- Pepper
- Salt

Directions:

- Heat oil in a pan over medium heat.
- Add onion and garlic to the pan and sauté for 5 minutes.
- Transfer sautéed onion and garlic to the soup maker along with remaining ingredients.
- Seal the soup maker with its lid and cook for 15 minutes on blend mode.
- Serve and enjoy.

Nutritional Value (Amount per Serving):

- Calories 373
- Fat 20.7 g
- Carbohydrates 42.3 g
- Sugar 4.8 g
- Protein 20.7 g
- Cholesterol 0 mg

31-Garlic Squash Cauliflower Soup

Time: 37 minutes

Serve: 6

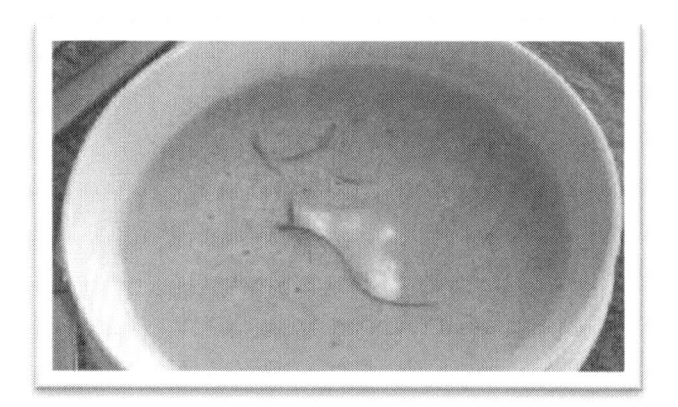

Ingredients:

- 1 lb butternut squash, cubed
- 2 cups of chicken stock
- 1 tsp paprika
- 2 tsp olive oil
- 3 garlic cloves, minced
- 1 lb cauliflower, chopped
- 1/2 tsp dried thyme
- 1/4 tsp red pepper flakes
- 1 onion, diced
- 1/2 cup heavy cream
- 1/2 tsp salt

Directions:

- Heat oil in a pan over medium heat.
- Add garlic and onion to the pan and sauté for 5 minutes.
- Add red pepper flakes, thyme, and paprika to the pan and sauté for minutes.
- Transfer pan mixture to the soup maker along with remaining ingredients.
- Seal the soup maker with its lid and cook on smooth mode.
- Serve and enjoy.

Nutritional Value (Amount per Serving):

- Calories 115
- Fat 5.7 g
- Carbohydrates 15.9 g
- Sugar 4.6 g
- Protein 3.1 g
- Cholesterol 0 mg

32-Thyme Nutmeg Squash Soup

Time: 35 minutes

Serve: 6

Ingredients:

- 6 cups of butternut squash, peeled and cubed
- 1/8 tsp nutmeg
- 2 tbsp olive oil
- 1/8 tsp cayenne pepper
- 2 tsp thyme
- 1/4 cup heavy cream
- 3 cups of vegetable stock
- 1 onion, chopped
- Pepper
- Salt

Directions:

- Heat oil in a pan over medium heat.
- Add onion to the pan and sauté for 3-4 minutes.
- Transfer sautéed onion to the soup maker along with remaining ingredients.
- Seal the soup maker with its lid and cook on smooth mode.
- Serve and enjoy.

Nutritional Value (Amount per Serving):

- Calories 134
- Fat 7 g
- Carbohydrates 18.9 g
- Sugar 4.2 g
- Protein 2.1 g
- Cholesterol 0 mg

33-Yummy Tomato Basil Soup

Time: 36 minutes

Serve: 6

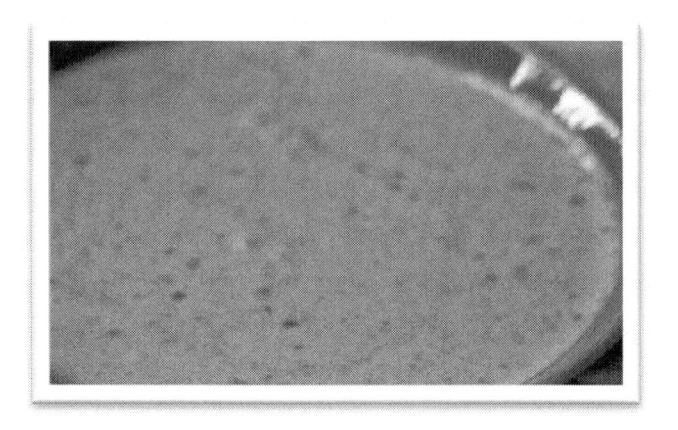

Ingredients:

- 28 oz can tomatoes
- 1 cup celery, diced
- 3 1/2 cups of chicken stock
- 1 cup onion, diced
- 1/3 cup cheddar cheese, grated
- 2 bay leaves
- 1 tbsp butter
- 2 tbsp olive oil
- 1 3/4 cup coconut milk
- 1/2 cup fresh basil, chopped
- 1 fresh thyme sprig
- 1 cup carrots, diced
- Pepper
- Salt

Directions:

- Heat butter and oil in a pan over medium heat.
- Add onion, carrots, and celery to the pan and sauté for 5 minutes.
- Transfer sautéed pan mixture to the soup maker along with remaining ingredients.
- Seal the soup maker with its lid and cook on smooth mode.
- Serve and enjoy.

Nutritional Value (Amount per Serving):

- Calories 296
- Fat 25.8 g
- Carbohydrates 15.3 g
- Sugar 9.2 g
- Protein 5.3 g
- Cholesterol 0 mg

34-Cabbage Tomato Soup

Time: 27 minutes

Serve: 4

Ingredients:

- 3 cups of cabbage, chopped
- 1/2 onion, sliced
- 2 tbsp olive oil
- 6 oz tomato paste
- 13 oz can stewed tomatoes
- 4 cups of water
- 4 garlic cloves, diced
- 13 oz can tomatoes, diced
- 1/4 tsp pepper
- 1 1/2 tsp salt

Directions:

- Heat oil in a pan over medium heat.
- Add garlic and onion the pan and sauté for 2 minutes.
- Transfer sautéed onion and garlic to the soup maker.
- Add remaining ingredients to the soup maker.
- Seal the soup maker with its lid and cook on chunky mode for 15 minutes.
- Season soup with salt and pepper.
- Serve and enjoy.

Nutritional Value (Amount per Serving):

- Calories 162
- Fat 7.5 g
- Carbohydrates 23.8 g
- Sugar 13.8 g
- Protein 4.5 g
- Cholesterol 0 mg

35-Asparagus Bacon Soup

Time: 35 minutes

Serve: 4

Ingredients:

- 25 asparagus spears, trimmed and cut into pieces
- 3 cups of vegetable stock
- 1 tbsp olive oil
- 5 bacon slices, cooked and chopped
- 1 medium onion, chopped
- Pepper
- Salt

Directions:

- Heat oil in a pan over medium heat.
- Add onion to the pot and sauté for 2-3 minutes.
- Transfer sautéed onion to the soup maker.
- Add remaining ingredients except for bacon.
- Seal the soup maker with its lid and cook on smooth mode.

- Add bacon and stir well.
- Serve and enjoy.

Nutritional Value (Amount per Serving):

- Calories 228
- Fat 14.7 g
- Carbohydrates 9.4 g
- Sugar 4.5 g
- Protein 16 g
- Cholesterol 0 mg

36-Celery Coconut Soup

Time: 30 minutes

Serve: 4

Ingredients:

- 6 cups of celery stalk, chopped
- 1 cup of coconut milk
- 1 medium onion, chopped
- 2 cups of chicken broth
- 1/2 tsp dill
- 1/4 tsp salt

Directions:

- Add all the ingredients to the soup maker.
- Cover soup maker with lid and cook for 25 minutes on blend mode.
- Season soup with salt and pepper.
- Serve and enjoy.

Nutritional Value (Amount per Serving):

- Calories 193
- Fat 15 g
- Carbohydrates 10.9 g
- Sugar 5.6 g
- Protein 5.2 g
- Cholesterol 0 mg

37-Spinach Broccoli Soup

Time: 37 minutes

Serve: 6

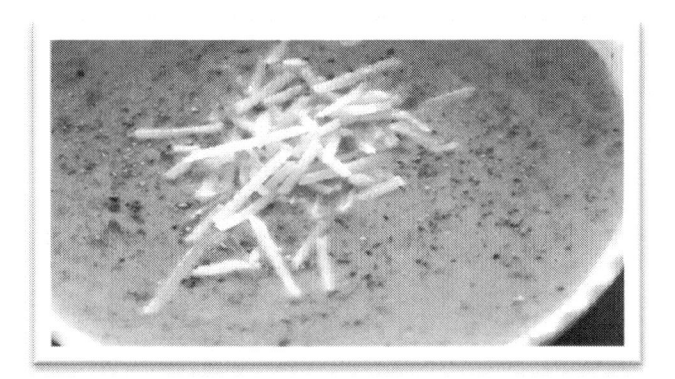

Ingredients:

- 2 cups of spinach
- 1 onion, chopped
- 4 cups of chicken broth
- 1 1/2 tsp dry mustard
- 2 garlic cloves, minced
- 2 tbsp olive oil
- 4 cups of broccoli florets
- 1/2 cup parmesan cheese, shredded
- 1 cup cheddar cheese, shredded
- 1 1/2 tsp salt

Directions:

- Heat oil in a pan over medium heat.
- Add onion, garlic, and spices to the pan and sauté for 2 minutes.
- Transfer sautéed mixture to the soup maker along with broccoli and broth.
- Seal the soup maker with its lid and cook on smooth mode.
- Add spinach and cook for 3-4 minutes on blend mode.
- Add cheese and stir well.
- Serve and enjoy.

Nutritional Value (Amount per Serving):

- Calories 232
- Fat 16 g
- Carbohydrates 8 g
- Sugar 2.5 g
- Protein 15.4 g
- Cholesterol 0 mg

38-Pumpkin Coconut Soup

Time: 31 minutes

Serve: 6

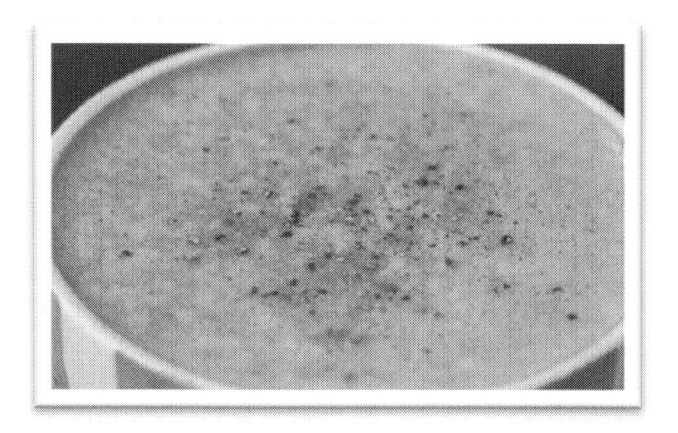

Ingredients:

- 2 cups of pumpkin puree
- 1 onion, chopped
- 2 cups of chicken broth
- 1/4 tsp nutmeg
- 2 cups of coconut milk
- 1/4 cup bell pepper, chopped
- 1/8 tsp thyme, dried
- 1/2 tsp salt

Directions:

- Add remaining ingredients to the soup maker.
- Cover soup maker with lid and cook on smooth mode.
- Season soup with salt and pepper.
- Serve warm and enjoy.

Nutritional Value (Amount per Serving):

- Calories 234
- Fat 19.8 g
- Carbohydrates 13.5 g
- Sugar 6.7 g
- Protein 4.6 g
- Cholesterol 0 mg

39-Easy Zucchini Soup

Time: 25 minutes

Serve: 6

Ingredients:

- 10 cups of zucchini, chopped
- 32 oz chicken broth
- 13 oz coconut milk
- 1 tbsp Thai curry paste

Directions:

- Add all the ingredients to the soup maker.
- Seal the soup maker with its lid and cook on blend mode for 15 minutes.
- Season soup with salt and pepper.
- Serve and enjoy.

Nutritional Value (Amount per Serving):

- Calories 198
- Fat 15.8 g
- Carbohydrates 10.8 g
- Sugar 5.9 g
- Protein 6.7 g
- Cholesterol 0 mg

40-Coconut Curried Carrot Soup

Time: 36 minutes

Serve: 4

Ingredients:

- 1 1/4 lbs carrot, chopped
- 1/2 tsp curry powder
- 1 jalapeno pepper, chopped
- 1 medium onion, chopped
- 1/2 cup coconut milk
- 1/4 tsp cayenne pepper
- 1/4 tsp turmeric
- 1/4 tsp garam masala
- 4 cups of chicken broth
- 2 tsp ginger, grated
- 1 tbsp olive oil
- 1 tsp garlic powder
- 1 tsp sea salt

Directions:

- Heat oil in a pan over medium heat.
- Add onion to the pan and sauté for 5 minutes.
- Add pepper and carrot and sauté for a minute.
- Transfer sautéed mixture to the soup maker along with remaining ingredients except for coconut milk.
- Seal the soup maker with its lid and cook on smooth mode.
- Add coconut milk and stir well.
- Serve and enjoy.

Nutritional Value (Amount per Serving):

- Calories 215
- Fat 12.2 g
- Carbohydrates 20.7 g
- Sugar 10.2 g
- Protein 7.3 g
- Cholesterol 0 mg

41-Celery Chicken Soup

Time: 33 minutes

Serve: 6

Ingredients:

- 2 chicken breast, skinless, boneless, and cut into chunks
- 2 celery stalks, diced
- 4 cups of chicken broth
- 2 carrots, diced
- 1/2 onion, diced
- 14 oz coconut milk

Directions:

- Add all the ingredients to the soup maker.
- Seal the soup maker with its lid and cook on chunky mode.
- Season soup with salt and pepper.
- Serve and enjoy.

Nutritional Value (Amount per Serving):

- Calories 229
- Fat 17.5 g
- Carbohydrates 7.3 g
- Sugar 4.1 g
- Protein 12.1 g
- Cholesterol 0 mg

42-Italian Cabbage Soup

Time: 38 minutes

Serve: 4

Ingredients:

- 1/2 cabbage head, chopped
- 1 tsp Creole seasoning
- 1 tsp Italian seasoning
- 4 cups of chicken broth
- 1 bell pepper, diced
- 3 celery ribs, diced
- 2 leeks, chopped
- 1 garlic clove, minced
- 2 carrots, diced
- 2 cups of mixed salad greens
- Pepper
- Salt

Directions:

- Add all the ingredients except salad greens in soup maker.
- Seal the soup maker with its lid and cook on chunky mode.
- Add salad green and stir until it wilts.
- Season soup with salt and pepper.
- Serve and enjoy.

Nutritional Value (Amount per Serving):

- Calories 191
- Fat 9.1 g
- Carbohydrates 21.2 g
- Sugar 8.8 g
- Protein 8.3 g
- Cholesterol 0 mg

43-Creamy Broccoli Carrot Soup

Time: 40 minutes

Serve: 4

Ingredients:

- 2 cups of broccoli florets, chopped
- 32 oz chicken broth
- 1 onion, diced
- 1 1/2 cup heavy whipping cream
- 2 tbsp olive oil
- 2 small carrots, diced
- 2 celery stalk, sliced
- 1/2 tsp pepper
- 1/2 tsp salt

Directions:

- Heat oil in a pan over medium heat.
- Add celery, carrots, and onion to the pan and sauté for 5 minutes.

- Transfer sautéed mixture to the soup maker along with remaining ingredients except for cream.
- Seal the soup maker with its lid and cook on blend mode for 25 minutes.
- Add cream and stir well.
- Season soup with salt and pepper.
- Serve and enjoy.

Nutritional Value (Amount per Serving):

- Calories 290
- Fat 25 g
- Carbohydrates 10.6 g
- Sugar 4 g
- Protein 7.4 g
- Cholesterol 0 mg

44-Chicken Spinach Mushroom Soup

Time: 35 minutes

Serve: 6

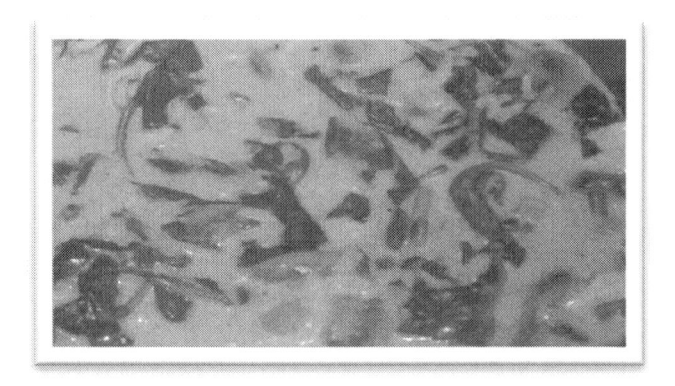

Ingredients:

- 1 lb chicken thighs, skinless, boneless, and cut into chunks
- 4 oz baby spinach
- 1/2 onion, diced
- 1 cup mushrooms, sliced
- 1 tsp ginger, chopped
- 3 garlic cloves, crushed
- 1/2 tsp turmeric
- 1 1/2 cups of coconut milk
- 1/4 cup cilantro, chopped
- 1 tsp garam masala
- 1/2 tsp cayenne pepper
- 1 tsp salt

Directions:

- Add all the ingredients to the soup maker.
- Seal the soup maker with its lid and cook on chunky mode.
- Serve and enjoy.

Nutritional Value (Amount per Serving):

- Calories 297
- Fat 20.1 g
- Carbohydrates 6.2 g
- Sugar 2.7 g
- Protein 24.4 g
- Cholesterol 0 mg

45-Onion Soup

Time: 46 minutes

Serve: 6

Ingredients:

- 8 cups of onions, peeled and sliced
- 2 tbsp olive oil
- 1 tbsp balsamic vinegar
- 6 cups of chicken broth
- 1 tsp salt

Directions:

- Heat oil in a pan over medium heat.
- Add onion to the pan and sauté until softened, about 15 minutes.
- Transfer sautéed onion to the soup maker along with remaining ingredients.
- Seal the soup maker with its lid and cook on smooth mode.
- Serve and enjoy.

Nutritional Value (Amount per Serving):

- Calories 140
- Fat 6.2 g
- Carbohydrates 15.3 g
- Sugar 7.2 g
- Protein 6.5 g
- Cholesterol 0 mg

46-Sweet Potato Bean Soup

Time: 30 minutes

Serve: 4

Ingredients:

- 1 lb sweet potato, diced
- 14 oz can black beans, rinsed
- 1/2 lime juice
- 1 cube chicken stock
- 3 cups of water
- 2 cups of tomatoes, chopped
- 1/2 red chili, sliced
- 3 garlic cloves, diced
- 2 tbsp olive oil
- 2 tsp ground cumin
- 2 tbsp fresh cilantro, chopped
- 1 tsp paprika
- 1 tsp ground coriander
- 1 onion, diced
- 2 tsp salt

Directions:

- Heat oil in a pan over medium heat.
- Add onion to the pan and sauté for 5 minutes.
- Transfer sautéed onion to the soup maker along with remaining ingredients.
- Seal the soup maker with its lid and cook on chunky mode.
- Serve and enjoy.

Nutritional Value (Amount per Serving):

- Calories 292
- Fat 8.2 g
- Carbohydrates 48.8 g
- Sugar 11.9 g
- Protein 9.3 g
- Cholesterol 0 mg

47-Kale Potato Soup

Time: 33 minutes

Serve: 6

Ingredients:

- 3 large potatoes, peeled and chopped
- 4 carrots, cut into pieces
- 4 cups of kale, chopped
- 6 cups of chicken broth
- Pepper
- Salt

Directions:

- Add all the ingredients except kale into the soup maker.
- Seal the soup maker with its lid and cook on chunky mode.
- Add kale and stir well and let sit for 5 minutes.
- Serve and enjoy.

Nutritional Value (Amount per Serving):

- Calories 204
- Fat 1.6 g
- Carbohydrates 38.6 g
- Sugar 4.8 g
- Protein 9.6 g
- Cholesterol 0 mg

48-Salsa Corn Bean Soup

Time: 33 minutes

Serve: 4

Ingredients:

- 4 cups of chicken stock
- 16 oz salsa
- 4 cups of can black beans
- 1 tsp cumin
- 2 cups of frozen corn
- 1 tsp chili powder
- 1 tsp salt

Directions:

- Add all the ingredients to the soup maker.
- Cover soup maker with lid and cook on chunky mode.
- Season soup with salt and pepper.
- Serve and enjoy.

Nutritional Value (Amount per Serving):

- Calories 350
- Fat 2.9 g
- Carbohydrates 68.9 g
- Sugar 8.7 g
- Protein 19.1 g
- Cholesterol 0 mg

49-Pea Carrot Soup

Time: 43 minutes

Serve: 6

Ingredients:

- 2 cups of yellow split peas, soak in hot water for 30 minutes
- 5 medium carrots, peeled and sliced
- 1 tsp turmeric
- 2 tbsp olive oil
- 6 cups of water
- 3 cups of ham, cut into cube
- 1 tsp coriander
- 1 tsp chili powder
- 1/2 tsp salt

Directions:

- Heat oil in a pan over medium heat.
- Add ham to the pan and sauté for 10 minutes.
- Transfer sautéed ham to the soup maker along with remaining ingredients.
- Seal the soup maker with its lid and cook on chunky mode.
- Stir well and serve.

Nutritional Value (Amount per Serving):

- Calories 397
- Fat 11.4 g
- Carbohydrates 47.7 g
- Sugar 7.8 g
- Protein 27.8 g
- Cholesterol 0 mg

50-Potato Carrot Soup

Time: 43 minutes

Serve: 4

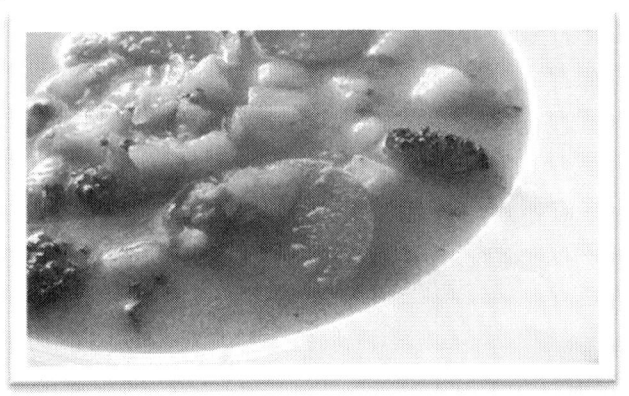

Ingredients:

- 3 cups of red potatoes, cubed
- 1 medium onion, diced
- 2 garlic cloves, chopped
- 1 tbsp olive oil
- 3 cups of chicken broth
- 1 medium carrot, diced
- 1 tsp pepper

Directions:

- Heat oil in a pan over medium heat.
- Add garlic, onion, and potatoes to the pan and sauté for 5 minutes.
- Transfer sautéed mixture to the soup maker.
- Add remaining ingredients to the soup maker.
- Seal the soup maker with its lid and cook on chunky mode.
- Serve and enjoy.

Nutritional Value (Amount per Serving):

- Calories 158
- Fat 4.8 g
- Carbohydrates 23.5 g
- Sugar 3.6 g
- Protein 6.4 g
- Cholesterol 0 mg

51-White Bean Carrot Soup

Time: 45 minutes

Serve: 4

Ingredients:

- 14 oz can white beans, rinsed and drained
- 3 cups of chicken stock
- 1 garlic cloves, minced
- 1 onion, diced
- 14 oz can tomatoes crushed, drained
- 1 carrot, diced
- 2 celery stalks, diced
- 2 tbsp olive oil
- Pepper
- Salt

Directions:

- Heat oil in a pan over medium heat.
- Add celery, onion, garlic, and carrot to the pan and sauté until softened.
- Transfer sautéed mixture to the soup maker along with remaining ingredients.
- Seal the soup maker with its lid and cook on chunky mode.
- Season soup with salt and pepper.
- Serve and enjoy.

Nutritional Value (Amount per Serving):

- Calories 291
- Fat 8.4 g
- Carbohydrates 46.7 g
- Sugar 3.3 g
- Protein 12.9 g
- Cholesterol 0 mg

52-Healthy Red Lentil Carrot Soup

Time: 45 minutes

Serve: 4

Ingredients:

- 1 cup red lentils, rinsed and soaked in water for 30 minutes
- 2 tsp ground coriander
- 2 tsp ground cumin
- 1/8 tsp cayenne
- 2 carrots, sliced
- 1 tbsp tomato paste
- 5 cups of vegetable stock
- 1 tsp ginger, grated
- 2 garlic cloves, crushed
- 1 onion, chopped
- 2 celery stalks, sliced
- 1 tbsp olive oil
- Pepper
- Salt

Directions:

- Heat oil in a pan over medium heat.
- Add garlic, ginger, celery, and onion to the pan and sauté for 5 minutes.
- Transfer sautéed mixture to the soup maker along with remaining ingredients.
- Seal the soup maker with its lid and cook on chunky mode.
- Serve and enjoy.

Nutritional Value (Amount per Serving):

- Calories 248
- Fat 6.9 g
- Carbohydrates 39.3 g
- Sugar 6.8 g
- Protein 13.5 g
- Cholesterol 0 mg

53-Cabbage Pork Soup

Time: 45 minutes

Serve: 2

Ingredients:

- ½ lb ground pork
- ½ tsp ground ginger
- 2 cup chicken stock
- 1 cup carrot, peeled and shredded
- 1 small onion, chopped
- 1 tbsp olive oil
- 1 ½ cup cabbage, chopped
- 1 tbsp soy sauce
- Pepper
- Salt

Directions:

- Heat oil in a pan over medium heat.
- Add meat to the pan and sauté for 3-4 minutes.
- Transfer meat to the soup maker along with remaining ingredients.
- Seal the soup maker with its lid and cook on chunky mode.
- Season soup with salt and pepper.
- Serve and enjoy.

Nutritional Value (Amount per Serving):

- Calories 288
- Fat 11.7 g
- Carbohydrates 13.4 g
- Sugar 6.7 g
- Protein 32.4 g
- Cholesterol 83 mg

54-Turmeric Tomato Soup

Time: 31 minutes

Serve: 4

Ingredients:

- 6 tomatoes, quartered
- 1 tsp garlic, minced
- ¼ cup coriander leaves, chopped
- 1 onion, diced
- 14 oz can coconut milk
- 1 tsp turmeric
- ½ tsp cayenne pepper
- 1 tsp ginger, minced
- Pepper
- Salt

Directions:

- Add all the ingredients to the soup maker.
- Seal the soup maker with its lid and cook on smooth mode.
- Season soup with salt and pepper.
- Serve and enjoy.

Nutritional Value (Amount per Serving):

- Calories 245
- Fat 21.7 g
- Carbohydrates 13.6 g
- Sugar 6.1 g
- Protein 4.1 g
- Cholesterol 0 mg

55-Chicken Tomato Soup

Time: 38 minutes

Serve: 6

Ingredients:

- 1 lb chicken thighs, boneless and cut into chunks
- 1 tsp turmeric powder
- 1 tbsp chicken broth base
- 10 oz Rotel can tomatoes
- 1 cup of coconut milk
- 2 cups of Swiss chard, chopped
- 1 ½ cups of celery stalks, chopped
- 1 oz ginger
- 5 garlic cloves
- 1 onion

Directions:

- Add onion, garlic, ginger, tomatoes, broth base, and half coconut milk into the blender and blend until smooth.
- Transfer blended mixture into the soup maker.
- Add chicken, celery, and Swiss chard to the soup maker.
- Seal the soup maker with its lid and cook on chunky mode.
- Add remaining coconut milk and stir well.
- Serve and enjoy.

Nutritional Value (Amount per Serving):

- Calories 283
- Fat 15.7 g
- Carbohydrates 12 g
- Sugar 4.4 g
- Protein 24.4 g
- Cholesterol 0 mg

56-Zesty Tomato Cabbage Soup

Time: 38 minutes

Serve: 8

Ingredients:

- 13 oz can tomatoes, diced
- 2 tbsp butter
- 6 oz tomato paste
- 13 oz can stewed tomatoes
- 4 cups of water
- 1/4 tsp pepper
- 3 cups of cabbage, chopped
- 1/2 onion, sliced
- 4 garlic cloves, diced
- 1 1/2 tsp salt

Directions:

- Melt butter in a pan over medium heat.
- Add garlic and onion to the pan and sauté for 2 minutes. Transfer to the soup maker.
- Add tomatoes, tomato paste, water, and cabbage to the soup maker.
- Seal the soup maker with its lid and cook on chunky mode.
- Season with salt and pepper.
- Serve and enjoy.

Nutritional Value (Amount per Serving):

- Calories 77
- Fat 3.1 g
- Carbohydrates 12 g
- Sugar 7 g
- Protein 2.4 g
- Cholesterol 0 mg

57-Chickpea Tomato Soup

Time: 45 minutes

Serve: 4

Ingredients:

- 14 oz can chickpeas, rinsed and drained
- 28 oz can tomatoes, crushed
- 3 cups of vegetable broth, low sodium
- 2 garlic cloves, minced
- 1/2 cup celery, diced
- 2 medium carrots, peeled and diced
- 1 medium onion, chopped
- 4 tbsp parmesan cheese, shredded
- 2 cups of fresh spinach
- 1 1/2 tbsp fresh basil, chopped
- 1 bay leaf
- 1 fresh rosemary spring
- 1 tsp olive oil
- 1/2 tsp pepper
- 1/2 tsp salt

Directions:

- Heat oil in a pan over medium heat.
- Add carrots, onion, garlic, and celery to the pan and sauté until softened.
- Transfer sautéed mixture to the soup maker along with remaining ingredients except for spinach.
- Seal the soup maker with its lid and cook on chunky mode.
- Add spinach and stir well.
- Serve and enjoy.

Nutritional Value (Amount per Serving):

- Calories 231
- Fat 3.5 g
- Carbohydrates 40.4 g
- Sugar 10.2 g
- Protein 11.6 g
- Cholesterol 0 mg

58-Healthy Vegetable Soup

Time: 38 minutes

Serve: 4

Ingredients:

- 1 small cabbage head, chopped
- 3 medium carrots, chopped
- 3 garlic cloves, chopped
- 28 oz can tomatoes, chopped
- 2 celery stalk, chopped
- 3 cups of vegetable broth, low sodium
- 1 tbsp fresh lemon juice
- 2 1/2 tbsp apple cider vinegar
- 1 medium onion, chopped

Directions:

- Add all the ingredients to the soup maker.
- Seal the soup maker with its lid and cook on chunky mode.
- Season soup with salt and pepper.
- Serve and enjoy.

Nutritional Value (Amount per Serving):

- Calories 117
- Fat 1.2 g
- Carbohydrates 21.1 g
- Sugar 12.1 g
- Protein 6.8 g
- Cholesterol 0 mg

59-Simple & Yummy Chicken Soup

Time: 38 minutes

Serve: 6

Ingredients:

- 1 1/2 lbs chicken thigh, skinless, boneless, and cut into chunks
- 8 oz Monterey cheese, shredded
- 15 oz chicken broth
- 15.5 oz chunky salsa

Directions:

- Add all the ingredients to the soup maker.
- Seal the soup maker with its lid and cook on chunky mode.
- Season soup with salt and pepper.
- Serve warm and enjoy.

Nutritional Value (Amount per Serving):

- Calories 400
- Fat 22 g
- Carbohydrates 7 g
- Sugar 3 g
- Protein 38 g
- Cholesterol 137 mg

60-Creamy Vegetable Soup

Time: 36 minutes

Serve: 4

Ingredients:

- ¼ cup of coconut milk
- 1 tsp thyme
- 3 cups of vegetable stock
- 2 garlic cloves, chopped
- 1 lb potatoes, peeled and chopped
- ¼ tsp red pepper flakes
- 1 tbsp olive oil
- 3 celery stalk, chopped
- 1 lb carrots, peeled and chopped
- 1 onion, chopped
- Pepper
- Salt

Directions:

- Heat oil in a pan over medium heat.
- Add carrot, onion, and celery to the pan and sauté until onion is softened.
- Transfer sautéed mixture to the soup maker along with remaining ingredients except for coconut milk.
- Seal the soup maker with its lid and cook on smooth mode.
- Add coconut milk and stir well. Season with salt and pepper.
- Serve and enjoy.

Nutritional Value (Amount per Serving):

- Calories 208
- Fat 7.8 g
- Carbohydrates 34 g
- Sugar 9.3 g
- Protein 3.7 g
- Cholesterol 0 mg

61-Creamy Basil Zucchini Soup

Time: 41 minutes

Serve: 4

Ingredients:

- 2 lbs zucchini, chopped
- 1/4 cup basil leaves
- 3 cups of vegetable stock
- 1 tbsp olive oil
- 2 garlic cloves, minced
- 3/4 cup onion, chopped
- 1 tsp salt

Directions:

- Heat olive oil in a pan over medium heat.
- Add garlic and onion and sauté for 5 minutes.
- Add zucchini and salt and cook for 5 minutes.
- Transfer sautéed mixture to the soup maker along with remaining ingredients.

- Seal the soup maker with its lid and cook on smooth mode.
- Serve and enjoy.

Nutritional Value (Amount per Serving):

- Calories 80
- Fat 4.5 g
- Carbohydrates 10.7 g
- Sugar 5.4 g
- Protein 3.1 g
- Cholesterol 0 mg

62- Delicious Onion Soup

Time: 36 minutes

Serve: 6

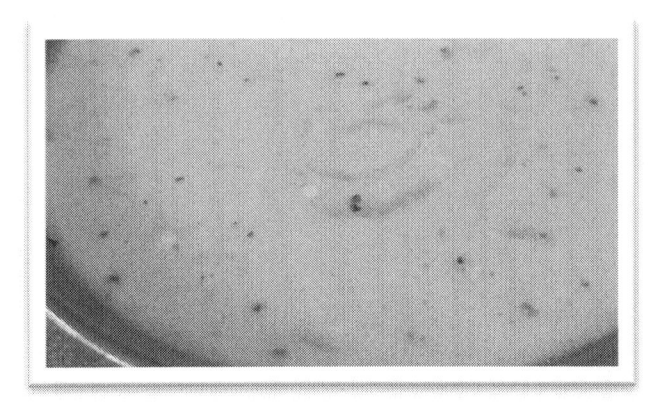

Ingredients:

- 17.5 oz onion, sliced
- 4 drops stevia
- 2 tbsp coconut oil
- 3 cups of vegetable stock
- 4 tbsp olive oil
- Pepper
- Salt

Directions:

- Heat coconut oil and olive oil in a pan over medium-low heat.
- Add onion to the pan and sauté for 5 minutes. Transfer to the soup maker.
- Add remaining ingredients to the soup maker.

- Seal the soup maker with its lid and cook on smooth mode.
- Season soup with salt and pepper.
- Serve and enjoy.

Nutritional Value (Amount per Serving):

- Calories 154
- Fat 14.3 g
- Carbohydrates 8.1 g
- Sugar 3.8 g
- Protein 0.9 g
- Cholesterol 0 mg

63-Brussels Sprout Soup

Time: 31 minutes

Serve: 6

Ingredients:

- 1 lb Brussels sprouts, cut the ends and halved
- ½ cup heavy cream
- 4 cups of chicken stock
- ½ tsp thyme
- 2 garlic cloves, minced
- 1/3 cup onion, chopped
- 1/3 cup carrot, chopped
- 1/3 cup celery, chopped
- ¼ tsp pepper
- 1/8 tsp salt

Directions:

- Add all the ingredients except cream into the soup maker.
- Seal the soup maker with its lid and cook on smooth mode.
- Add cream and stir well.
- Season with salt and pepper.
- Serve and enjoy.

Nutritional Value (Amount per Serving):

- Calories 82
- Fat 4.4 g
- Carbohydrates 9.5 g
- Sugar 2.8 g
- Protein 3.5 g
- Cholesterol 14 mg

64-Tomato Chickpea Soup

Time: 45 minutes

Serve: 4

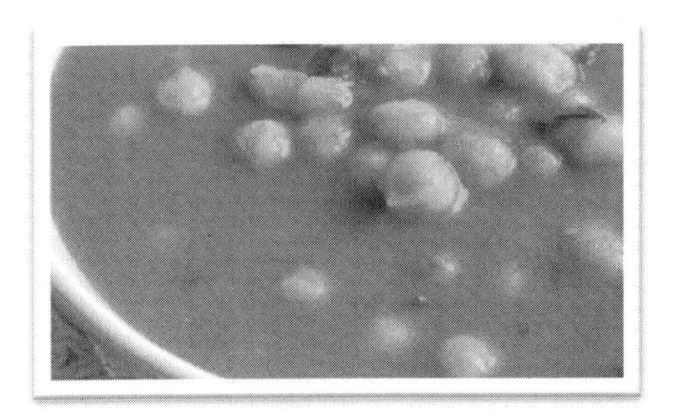

Ingredients:

- 14 oz can chickpeas
- 4 cups of vegetable stock
- 1 tbsp tomato paste
- 14 oz can tomatoes, chopped
- ¼ tsp onion powder
- ¼ tsp garlic powder
- 1 tsp oregano
- 1 tsp paprika
- 1 carrot, diced
- 2 garlic cloves, crushed
- 1 onion, diced
- Pepper
- Salt

Directions:

- Spray pan with cooking spray and heat over medium heat.
- Add onion and garlic to the pan and sauté for 5 minutes.
- Transfer sautéed onion and garlic to the soup maker along with remaining ingredients.
- Seal the soup maker with its lid and cook on chunky mode.
- Serve and enjoy.

Nutritional Value (Amount per Serving):

- Calories 168
- Fat 1.8 g
- Carbohydrates 34.1 g
- Sugar 6.5 g
- Protein 6.7 g
- Cholesterol 0 mg

65-Eastern Lentil Soup

Time: 31 minutes

Serve: 4

Ingredients:

- 1 ½ cups of red split lentils, rinsed and soaked in water for 30 minutes
- 1 tsp turmeric
- 1 tsp ground cumin
- 6 ½ cups of water
- 2 tbsp olive oil
- 1 small onion, chopped
- ½ tsp black pepper
- 1 tsp salt

Directions:

- Heat oil in a pan over medium heat.
- Add onion to the pan and sauté until softened.
- Transfer sautéed onion to the soup maker.
- Add remaining ingredients to the soup maker.
- Cover soup maker with lid and cook on smooth mode.

- Season soup with salt and pepper.
- Serve and enjoy.

Nutritional Value (Amount per Serving):

- Calories 267
- Fat 8 g
- Carbohydrates 33.9 g
- Sugar 2.3 g
- Protein 15.4 g
- Cholesterol 0 mg

66-Avocado Soup

Time: 36 minutes

Serve: 4

Ingredients:

- 2 avocados, peeled and mashed
- ¼ cup fresh cilantro, chopped
- ¼ tsp ground cumin
- 2 cups of heavy cream
- 1 tsp fresh lime juice
- 4 cups of chicken stock
- 1 garlic clove, minced
- ½ cup onion, chopped
- 1 tbsp butter
- Pepper
- Salt

Directions:

- Melt butter in a pan over medium heat.
- Add garlic and onion to the pan and sauté for 5 minutes.
- Transfer sautéed onion and garlic to the soup maker along with remaining ingredients except for cream.
- Seal the soup maker with its lid and cook on smooth mode.
- Add cream and stir well.
- Season with salt and pepper.
- Serve and enjoy.

Nutritional Value (Amount per Serving):

- Calories 283
- Fat 28.2 g
- Carbohydrates 6.5 g
- Sugar 1.6 g
- Protein 2.7 g
- Cholesterol 90 mg

67-Tomato White Bean Soup

Time: 36 minutes

Serve: 4

Ingredients:

- 1 lb can white beans
- 2 garlic cloves, minced
- 1 onion, chopped
- 14 oz can tomatoes
- ½ tsp ground coriander
- ½ tsp ground cumin
- ½ tsp chili powder
- 1 tbsp olive oil
- 6 ½ cups of hot water
- Pepper
- Salt

Directions:

- Heat oil in a pan over medium heat.
- Add garlic and onion and sauté until onion is softened.
- Add spices and sauté for a minute.
- Transfer sautéed onion mixture to the soup maker.
- Add remaining ingredients to the soup maker and stir well.
- Cover soup maker with lid and cook on smooth mode.
- Season soup with salt and pepper.
- Serve and enjoy.

Nutritional Value (Amount per Serving):

- Calories 179
- Fat 4 g
- Carbohydrates 32.5 g
- Sugar 4.9 g
- Protein 9.6 g
- Cholesterol 0 mg

68-Apple Sweet Potato Soup

Time: 31 minutes

Serve: 4

Ingredients:

- 1/2 lb apples, cored and chopped
- 1/2 cup coconut milk
- 1/2 tbsp apple cider vinegar
- 16 oz vegetable stock
- 1/2 tsp turmeric
- 1/4 lb potatoes, peeled and diced
- 1 lb sweet potatoes, peeled and diced
- 2 garlic cloves, peeled
- ½ onion, diced
- Pepper
- Salt

Directions:

- Add all the ingredients except coconut milk into the soup maker.
- Seal the soup maker with its lid and cook on smooth mode.
- Add coconut milk and stir well.
- Season with salt and pepper.
- Serve and enjoy.

Nutritional Value (Amount per Serving):

- Calories 253
- Fat 7.6 g
- Carbohydrates 44.6 g
- Sugar 6.2 g
- Protein 3.7 g
- Cholesterol 0 mg

69-Cinnamon Apple Squash Soup

Time: 31 minutes

Serve: 8

Ingredients:

- 1 medium butternut squash, peeled, seeded and diced
- 1 apple, cored and diced
- 1/2 cup can coconut milk
- 1/8 tsp ground cinnamon
- 1 carrot, peeled and diced
- 2 garlic cloves, minced
- 2 cups of vegetable stock
- 1/8 tsp cayenne
- 1/4 tsp black pepper
- 1 onion, diced
- 1/2 tsp salt

Directions:

- Add all the ingredients except coconut milk to the soup maker.
- Cover soup maker with lid and cook on smooth mode.
- Add coconut milk and stir well.
- Serve and enjoy.

Nutritional Value (Amount per Serving):

- Calories 74
- Fat 3.4 g
- Carbohydrates 12 g
- Sugar 4.5 g
- Protein 1.1 g
- Cholesterol 0 mg

70-Italian Chicken Soup

Time: 40 minutes

Serve: 6

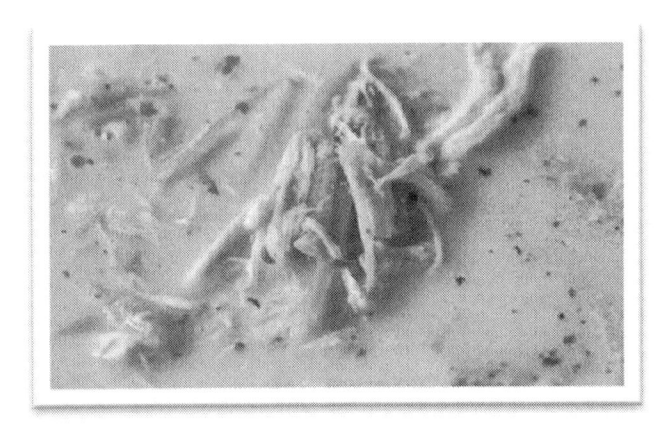

Ingredients:

- 1 1/2 lbs chicken breasts, skinless, boneless, and cut into chunks
- 1 tsp garlic powder
- 1 tbsp Italian seasoning
- 8 oz tomato sauce
- 14 oz tomatoes, diced
- 1 cup chicken broth
- 14 oz can coconut milk
- 1 large onion, chopped
- 1/4 tsp black pepper
- 1/2 tsp salt

Directions:

- Add all the ingredients to the soup maker.
- Cover soup maker with lid and cook on chunky mode.
- Season soup with salt and pepper.
- Serve and enjoy.

Nutritional Value (Amount per Serving):

- Calories 392
- Fat 23.7 g
- Carbohydrates 9.6 g
- Sugar 3 g
- Protein 36.4 g
- Cholesterol 103 mg

71-Simple Asparagus Soup

Time: 31 minutes

Serve: 4

Ingredients:

- 1 lb asparagus, wash, trimmed and chopped
- 1/4 tsp pepper
- 2 tbsp butter
- 1/2 cup onion, chopped
- 2 cups of chicken broth
- 1/2 tsp salt

Directions:

- Add all the ingredients to the soup maker.
- Seal the soup maker with its lid and cook on smooth mode.
- Season with salt and pepper.
- Serve and enjoy.

Nutritional Value (Amount per Serving):

- Calories 99
- Fat 6.6 g
- Carbohydrates 6.3 g
- Sugar 3 g
- Protein 5.1 g
- Cholesterol 15 mg

72-Mushroom Cauliflower Soup

Time: 31 minutes

Serve: 3

Ingredients:

- 1 1/2 cups of mushrooms, diced
- 1/2 onion, chopped
- 1/2 tsp olive oil
- 2 cups of cauliflower florets
- 1 tsp onion powder
- 1 2/3 cups of almond milk, unsweetened
- 1/4 tsp sea salt

Directions:

- Add all the ingredients to the soup maker and stir well.
- Cover soup maker with lid and cook on smooth mode.
- Season soup with salt and pepper.
- Serve hot and enjoy.

Nutritional Value (Amount per Serving):

- Calories 348
- Fat 32 g
- Carbohydrates 13 g
- Sugar 7 g
- Protein 5 g
- Cholesterol 0 mg

73-Cinnamon Broccoli Avocado Soup

Time: 31 minutes

Serve: 4

Ingredients:

- 1 small avocado, peel and chopped
- 4 cups of broccoli florets
- 2 cups of vegetable broth
- 1/2 tsp cinnamon
- Pepper
- Salt

Directions:

- Add all the ingredients to the soup maker.
- Seal the soup maker with its lid and cook on smooth mode.
- Season with salt and pepper.
- Serve and enjoy.

Nutritional Value (Amount per Serving):

- Calories 153
- Fat 10 g
- Carbohydrates 11 g
- Sugar 2 g
- Protein 6 g
- Cholesterol 0 mg

74-Cauliflower Leek Soup

Time: 31 minutes

Serve: 4

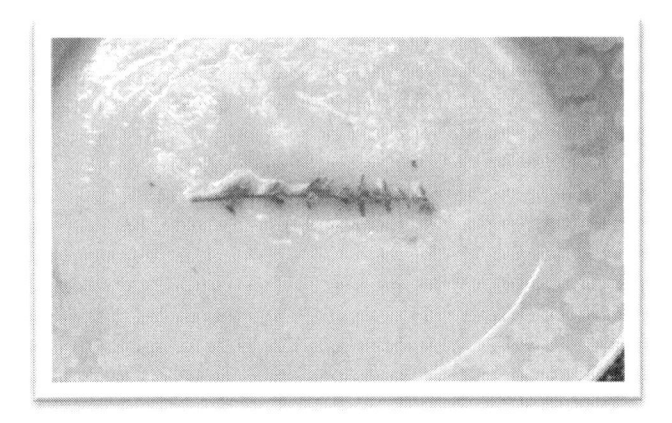

Ingredients:

- 1/2 cauliflower, chopped
- 1 large leek, chopped
- 3 cups of vegetable broth
- 1/2 cup coconut cream
- Salt

Directions:

- Add all the ingredients except coconut cream to the soup maker.
- Cover soup maker with lid and cook on smooth mode.
- Add coconut cream and stir well.
- Season soup with salt and pepper.
- Serve and enjoy.

Nutritional Value (Amount per Serving):

- Calories 129
- Fat 8 g
- Carbohydrates 9 g
- Sugar 4 g
- Protein 6 g
- Cholesterol 0 mg

75-Delicious Tomato Pumpkin Soup

Time: 20 minutes

Serve: 4

Ingredients:

- 1/2 cup tomato, chopped
- 2 cups of pumpkin
- 2 cups of vegetable broth, low-sodium
- 1 tsp olive oil
- 1/2 tsp garlic, minced
- 1 1/2 tsp curry powder
- 1/2 tsp paprika
- 1/2 cup onion, chopped

Directions:

- Add all the ingredients to the soup maker.
- Seal the soup maker with its lid and cook on blend mode for 10 minutes.
- Season with salt and pepper.
- Serve and enjoy.

Nutritional Value (Amount per Serving):

- Calories 84
- Fat 2 g
- Carbohydrates 13 g
- Sugar 5 g
- Protein 4 g
- Cholesterol 0 mg

76-Flavorful Herb Tomato Soup

Time: 31 minutes

Serve: 4

Ingredients:

- 3 cups of tomatoes, peeled, seeded and chopped
- 1 tbsp basil, chopped
- 1 cup red bell pepper, chopped
- 1 cup onion, chopped
- 2 tbsp tomato paste
- 4 cups of vegetable broth, low-sodium
- 1/2 tsp thyme, chopped
- 1 tsp fresh oregano, chopped
- 1 tbsp garlic, minced
- 1 tbsp olive oil
- 1/4 tsp pepper

Directions:

- Add all the ingredients to the soup maker.
- Seal the soup maker with its lid and cook on smooth mode.
- Season with salt and pepper.
- Serve and enjoy.

Nutritional Value (Amount per Serving):

- Calories 125
- Fat 5 g
- Carbohydrates 13 g
- Sugar 8 g
- Protein 7 g
- Cholesterol 0 mg

77-Kale Spinach Soup

Time: 20 minutes

Serve: 8

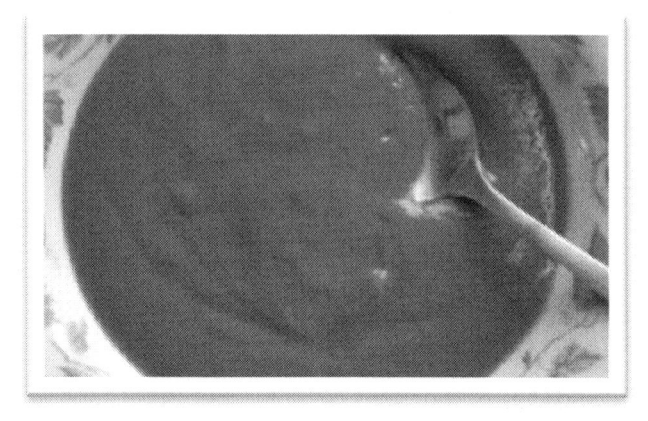

Ingredients:

- 1/2 lb fresh spinach
- 1/2 lb kale
- 2 avocados
- 1 fresh lime juice
- 3 oz olive oil
- 1 cup of water
- 3 1/3 cups of coconut milk
- 1/4 tsp pepper
- 1 tsp salt

Directions:

- Add all the ingredients to the soup maker and stir well.
- Cover soup maker with lid and cook on blend mode for 10 minutes.
- Season soup with salt and pepper.
- Serve warm and enjoy.

Nutritional Value (Amount per Serving):

- Calories 438
- Fat 43 g
- Carbohydrates 13 g
- Sugar 3 g
- Protein 5 g
- Cholesterol 0 mg

78-Coconut Celery Soup

Time: 31 minutes

Serve: 4

Ingredients:

- 6 cups of celery, diced
- 1/2 tsp dill
- 2 cups of water
- 1 cup of coconut milk
- 1 medium onion, diced
- 1/2 tsp sea salt

Directions:

- Add all the ingredients to the soup maker and stir well.
- Cover soup maker with lid and cook on smooth mode.
- Season soup with salt and pepper.
- Serve warm and enjoy.

Nutritional Value (Amount per Serving):

- Calories 174
- Fat 14 g
- Carbohydrates 10 g
- Sugar 5 g
- Protein 2 g
- Cholesterol 0 mg

79-Cauliflower Watercress Soup

Time: 31 minutes

Serve: 5

Ingredients:

- 5 watercress, chopped
- 8 cups of vegetable broth
- 1/2 cup of coconut milk
- 1 lb cauliflower, chopped
- 5 oz fresh spinach, chopped
- Salt

Directions:

- Add all the ingredients to the soup maker and stir well.
- Cover soup maker with lid and cook on smooth mode.
- Season soup with salt and pepper.
- Serve warm and enjoy.

Nutritional Value (Amount per Serving):

- Calories 153
- Fat 8 g
- Carbohydrates 8 g
- Protein 12 g
- Sugar 4 g
- Cholesterol 0 mg

80-Simple Asparagus Soup

Time: 31 minutes

Serve: 4

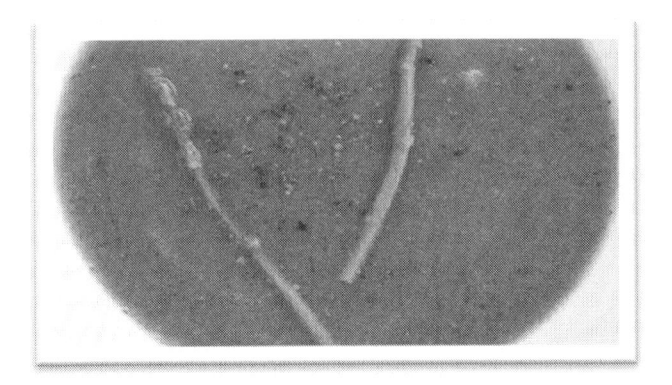

Ingredients:

- 1 lb zucchini, chopped
- 4 cups of Vegetable Broth
- 1 lb asparagus, trimmed and chopped
- Salt

Directions:

- Add all the ingredients to the soup maker.
- Cover soup maker with lid and cook on smooth mode.
- Serve and enjoy.

Nutritional Value (Amount per Serving):

- Calories 79
- Fat 2 g
- Carbohydrates 9 g
- Sugar 4 g
- Protein 8 g
- Cholesterol 0 mg

81-Brown Lentil Soup

Time: 31 minutes

Serve: 6

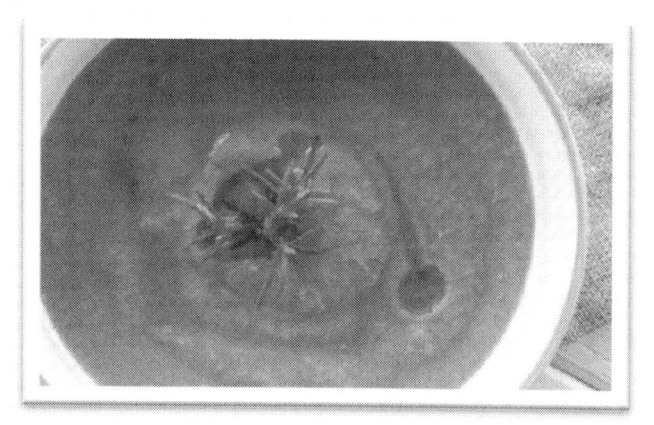

Ingredients:

- ½ cup brown lentils, rinsed and soaked in water for 30 minutes
- 1 large onion, chopped
- 2 garlic clove, minced
- 3 small carrots, diced
- 1/4 tsp ground cumin
- 3 cups of chicken stock
- 14 oz can tomatoes, crushed
- Pepper
- Salt

Directions:

- Add all the ingredients to the soup maker.
- Cover soup maker with lid and cook on smooth mode.
- Season soup with salt and pepper.
- Serve warm and enjoy.

Nutritional Value (Amount per Serving):

- Calories 96
- Fat 0.7 g
- Carbohydrates 18.4 g
- Sugar 4.9 g
- Protein 5.5 g
- Cholesterol 0 mg

82-Onion Shallot Soup

Time: 35 minutes

Serve: 4

Ingredients:

- 1 onion, sliced
- 1 leek, sliced
- 1 garlic clove, chopped
- 1 shallot, sliced
- 1 1/2 tbsp olive oil
- 4 cups of vegetable stock
- Salt

Directions:

- Add all the ingredients to the soup maker.
- Cover soup maker with lid and cook on blend mode for 25 minutes.
- Season soup with salt and pepper.
- Serve warm and enjoy.

Nutritional Value (Amount per Serving):

- Calories 82
- Fat 5 g
- Carbohydrates 8 g
- Sugar 2 g
- Protein 1 g
- Cholesterol 0 mg

83-Cheese Tomato Soup

Time: 36 minutes

Serve: 6

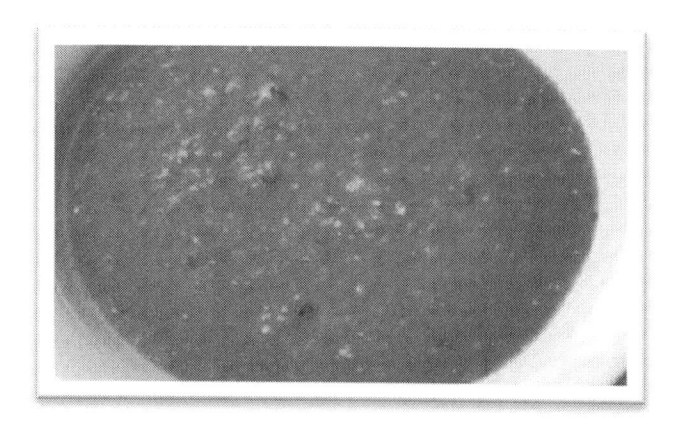

Ingredients:

- 14.5 oz can tomatoes, peeled
- 2/3 cup feta cheese, crumbled
- 1/3 cup heavy cream
- 3 cups of water
- 1 tsp erythritol
- 1 tsp dried basil
- 1/2 tsp dried oregano
- 1/8 tsp black pepper
- 2 garlic cloves, minced
- 1/4 cup onion, chopped
- 2 tbsp olive oil
- 1/2 tsp salt

Directions:

- Heat oil in a pan over medium heat.
- Add garlic and onion and sauté until onion is softened.
- Transfer sautéed onion and garlic to the soup maker along with remaining ingredients except for feta cheese.
- Seal the soup maker with its lid and cook on smooth mode.
- Add feta cheese and stir well.
- Serve and enjoy.

Nutritional Value (Amount per Serving):

- Calories 170
- Fat 13 g
- Carbohydrates 10 g
- Sugar 6 g
- Protein 4 g
- Cholesterol 43 mg

84-Creamy Mushroom Soup

Time: 31 minutes

Serve: 4

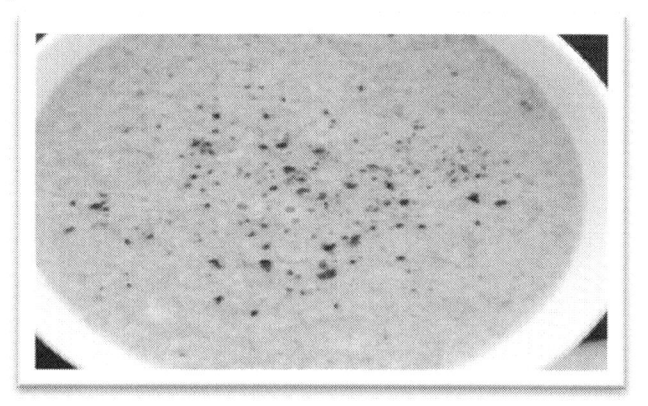

Ingredients:

- 8 oz mushrooms, washed and sliced
- 1/2 cup heavy whipping cream
- 2 cups of vegetable stock
- 2 tbsp butter
- 1/2 medium onion, chopped
- Salt

Directions:

- Melt butter in a pan over medium heat.
- Add onion to the pan and sauté until softened.
- Transfer sautéed onion to the soup maker along with remaining ingredients except for cream.
- Seal the soup maker with its lid and cook on smooth mode.
- Add cream and stir well. Season soup with salt and pepper.
- Serve and enjoy.

Nutritional Value (Amount per Serving):

- Calories 123
- Fat 12 g
- Carbohydrates 4.1 g
- Sugar 2.1 g
- Protein 2.3 g
- Cholesterol 36 mg

85-Cheddar Broccoli Soup

Time: 25 minutes

Serve: 6

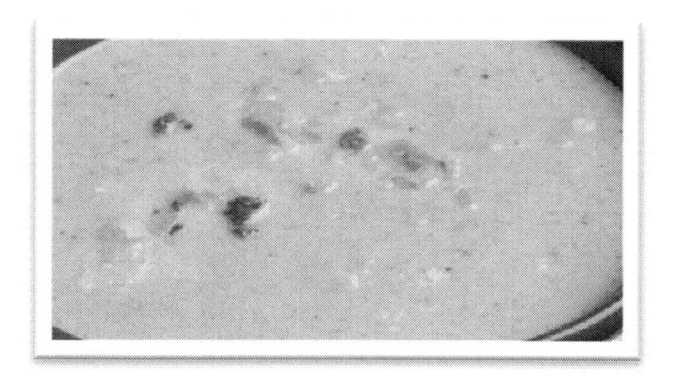

Ingredients:

- 8 cups of broccoli florets
- 2 cups of cheddar cheese, shredded
- 1 cup of heavy cream
- 4 cups of vegetable broth
- ¼ tsp black pepper
- 1 tsp salt

Directions:

- Add all the ingredients except cheese and cream into the soup maker.
- Seal the soup maker with its lid and cook on blend mode for 15 minutes.
- Add cheese and cream and stir well.
- Serve and enjoy.

Nutritional Value (Amount per Serving):

- Calories 288
- Fat 21.2 g
- Carbohydrates 9.8 g
- Sugar 2.7 g
- Protein 16.4 g
- Cholesterol 67 mg

86-Cauliflower Roasted Pepper Soup

Time: 34 minutes

Serve: 4

Ingredients:

- 1 cup of coconut milk
- 1/8 tsp fresh thyme
- 4 cups of vegetable broth
- 4 cups of cauliflower florets
- 1/4 tsp red pepper flakes
- 1 tsp paprika
- 1 tbsp seasoned salt
- 1 large shallot, chopped
- 1/2 cup roasted red pepper, chopped
- 2 tbsp coconut oil

Directions:

- Heat oil in a pan over medium heat.
- Add shallots and sauté for 3 minutes.
- Transfer shallots to the soup maker along with remaining ingredients except for coconut milk.
- Seal the soup maker with its lid and cook on smooth mode.
- Add coconut milk and stir well.
- Serve and enjoy.

Nutritional Value (Amount per Serving):

- Calories 245
- Fat 20.5 g
- Carbohydrates 10.4 g
- Sugar 4.2 g
- Protein 8.4 g
- Cholesterol 0 mg

87-Green Cauliflower Soup

Time: 40 minutes

Serve: 4

Ingredients:

- 4 cups of cauliflower florets, chopped
- 2 tbsp butter
- 1/2 cup coconut milk
- 2 cups of water
- 4 cups of vegetable broth
- 1 tsp curry powder
- 4 garlic cloves, minced
- 1 small onion, chopped
- 3 cups of baby spinach, chopped
- 1 bunch chard, chopped

Directions:

- Melt butter in a pan over medium heat.
- Add onion to the pan and sauté until softened.
- Add garlic and sauté for a minute.
- Transfer sautéed onion and garlic to the soup maker along with remaining ingredients except for coconut milk.
- Seal the soup maker with its lid and cook on smooth mode.
- Add coconut milk and stir well.
- Serve and enjoy.

Nutritional Value (Amount per Serving):

- Calories 211
- Fat 15.6 g
- Carbohydrates 12 g
- Sugar 5.1 g
- Protein 8.8 g
- Cholesterol 0 mg

88-Curried Summer Squash Soup

Time: 25 minutes

Serve: 4

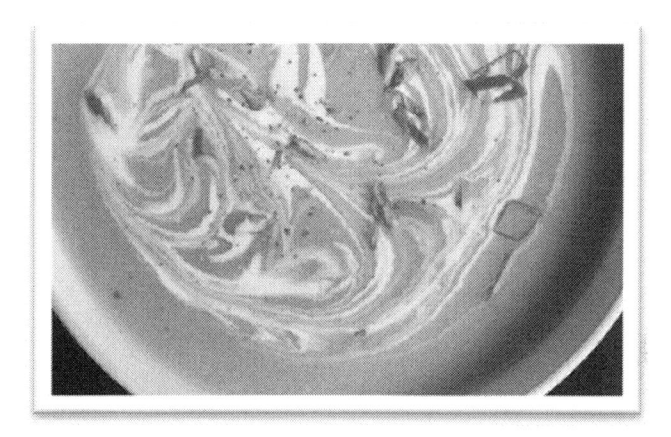

Ingredients:

- 1 1/2 lbs summer squash, ends trimmed and cut into 1-inch pieces
- 1/2 lime juice
- 1/4 cup coconut milk
- 4 cups of vegetable stock
- 3/4 tsp curry powder
- 1 garlic clove, minced
- 1 onion, chopped
- 1 tbsp olive oil
- Pepper
- Salt

Directions:

- Heat oil in a pan over medium heat.
- Add onion to the pan and sauté until softened.
- Transfer onion to the soup maker along with coconut milk and lime juice
- Seal the soup maker with its lid and cook on blend mode for 15 minutes.
- Add coconut milk and lime juice.
- Season with salt and pepper.
- Serve and enjoy.

Nutritional Value (Amount per Serving):

- Calories 114
- Fat 8.1 g
- Carbohydrates 11.5 g
- Sugar 8.3 g
- Protein 2.5 g
- Cholesterol 0 mg

89-Simple Potato Soup

Time: 33 minutes

Serve: 4

Ingredients:

- 28 oz potatoes, peeled and diced
- 32 oz chicken broth
- 1 packet gravy mix

Directions:

- Add all the ingredients to the soup maker.
- Cover soup maker with lid and cook on chunky mode.
- Serve warm and enjoy.

Nutritional Value (Amount per Serving):

- Calories 173
- Fat 1.5 g
- Carbohydrates 32 g
- Sugar 2.9 g
- Protein 7.9 g
- Cholesterol 0 mg

90-Sausage Potato Soup

Time: 45 minutes

Serve: 6

Ingredients:

- 4 potatoes, diced
- 4 cups of chicken broth
- 1 lb smoked sausage, sliced
- 2 carrots, diced
- 2 celery stalks, diced
- 1 onion, diced
- 3 bacon slices, cooked and diced
- Pepper
- Salt

Directions:

- Spray pan with cooking spray and heat over medium heat.
- Add onion to the pan and sauté until softened.
- Transfer sautéed onion to the soup maker along with remaining ingredients.
- Seal the soup maker with its lid and cook on chunky mode.
- Season with salt and pepper.
- Serve and enjoy.

Nutritional Value (Amount per Serving):

- Calories 396
- Fat 22.5 g
- Carbohydrates 26.8 g
- Sugar 4 g
- Protein 20.7 g
- Cholesterol 64 mg

91-Easy Tomato Soup

Time: 31 minutes

Serve: 6

Ingredients:

- 46 oz tomato juice
- ¼ cup of sugar
- ¼ tsp onion powder
- 1 tsp curry powder
- ¼ cup all-purpose flour
- ¼ cup butter
- Pepper
- Salt

Directions:

- Add all the ingredients to the soup maker.
- Cover soup maker with lid and cook on smooth mode.
- Season soup with salt and pepper.
- Serve warm and enjoy.

Nutritional Value (Amount per Serving):

- Calories 156
- Fat 7.9 g
- Carbohydrates 21.8 g
- Sugar 16.1 g
- Protein 2.3 g
- Cholesterol 20 mg

92-Cream of Mushroom Soup

Time: 38 minutes

Serve: 6

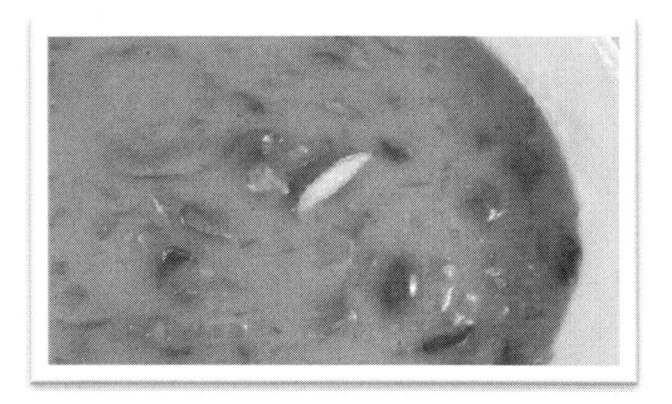

Ingredients:

- ½ lb mushrooms, sliced
- 1 cup half and half
- 28 oz chicken broth
- 6 tbsp flour
- 1 small onion, chopped
- 2 tbsp butter
- ¼ tsp pepper
- ½ tsp salt

Directions:

- Melt butter in a pan over medium heat.
- Add onion and mushroom to the pan sauté until onion is softened.
- Transfer onion-mushroom mixture to the soup maker.
- Add remaining ingredients to the soup maker.

- Cover soup maker with lid and cook on chunky mode.
- Season soup with salt and pepper.
- Serve and enjoy.

Nutritional Value (Amount per Serving):

- Calories 149
- Fat 9.4 g
- Carbohydrates 10.6 g
- Sugar 1.6 g
- Protein 6 g
- Cholesterol 25 mg

93-Healthy Red Lentil Soup

Time: 30 minutes

Serve: 4

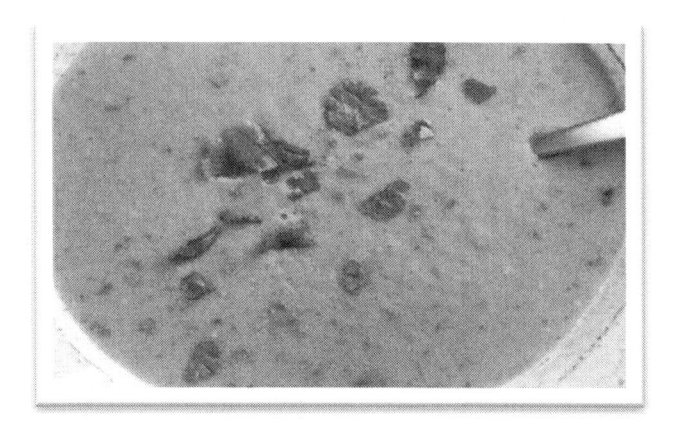

Ingredients:

- 1 cup red lentils, soaked and drained
- 1 onion, diced
- 1 cup carrots, diced
- 1 cup tomatoes, diced
- ½ tsp ginger garlic paste
- ¼ tsp turmeric powder
- 1/4 tsp chili powder
- 1 tsp salt

Directions:

- Add all the ingredients to the soup maker and stir well.
- Add water to the minimum mark.
- Cover soup maker with lid and cook on smooth mode.
- Season soup with salt and pepper.
- Garnish with cream and serve.

Nutritional Value (Amount per Serving):

- Calories 204
- Fat 0.8 g
- Carbohydrates 36.4 g
- Sugar 4.7 g
- Protein 13.5 g
- Cholesterol 0 mg

94-Turmeric Tomato Soup

Time: 35 minutes

Serve: 2

Ingredients:

- 5 oz cherry tomatoes, halved
- 14 oz tomatoes, diced
- 1 tbsp apple cider vinegar
- 1 tsp basil, dried
- 1 tsp coconut oil
- 2 tsp turmeric powder
- 2 garlic cloves, minced
- 1 small onion, diced
- 1/2 cup vegetable stock, low sodium
- 1/4 tsp pepper
- 1/2 tsp salt

Directions:

- Heat oil in a pan over medium heat.
- Add onion and garlic and sauté until softened.
- Transfer onion and garlic to the soup maker along with remaining ingredients.
- Seal the soup maker with its lid and cook on smooth mode.
- Season with salt and pepper.
- Serve and enjoy.

Nutritional Value (Amount per Serving):

- Calories 103
- Fat 3.7 g
- Carbohydrates 17.2 g
- Sugar 9 g
- Protein 3 g
- Cholesterol 0 mg

95-Healthy Anti-inflammatory Broccoli Soup

Time: 35 minutes

Serve: 6

Ingredients:

- 8 cups of broccoli florets
- 6 cups of vegetable broth, low sodium
- 1 tbsp sesame oil
- 1 tsp ground turmeric
- 2 tbsp ginger, chopped
- 4 cups of leeks, chopped
- 2 tbsp olive oil
- 1 tsp salt

Directions:

- Heat oil in a pan over medium heat.
- Add leek to the pan and sauté for 5 minutes.
- Transfer sautéed leek to the soup maker along with remaining ingredients.

- Seal the soup maker with its lid and cook on smooth mode.
- Serve and enjoy.

Nutritional Value (Amount per Serving):

- Calories 184
- Fat 9 g
- Carbohydrates 18.9 g
- Sugar 5.1 g
- Protein 9.3 g
- Cholesterol 0 mg

96-Green Vegetable Soup

Time: 36 minutes

Serve: 2

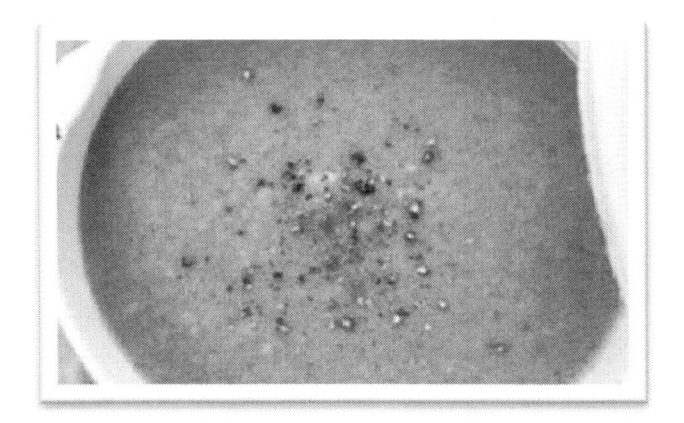

Ingredients:

- 1 cup fresh spinach
- 1 fennel bulb, diced
- 1/2 cup fresh kale leaves, chopped
- 1 small onion, diced
- 1/4 cup fresh asparagus, chopped
- 2 celery stalks, chopped
- 1 lime juice
- 1 tsp coconut oil
- 2 garlic cloves, minced
- 2 cup vegetable stock

Directions:

- Heat oil in a pan over medium heat.
- Add asparagus, fennel, celery, onion, and garlic to the pan and sauté for 5 minutes.
- Transfer sautéed vegetables to the soup maker along with remaining ingredients.
- Seal the soup maker with its lid and cook on smooth mode.
- Serve warm and enjoy.

Nutritional Value (Amount per Serving):

- Calories 103
- Fat 3.7 g
- Carbohydrates 19.1 g
- Sugar 3.5 g
- Protein 3.5 g
- Cholesterol 0 mg

97-Chunky Bean Vegetable Soup

Time: 45 minutes

Serve: 6

Ingredients:

- 1 bunch kale, chopped
- 15 oz can northern beans, rinsed and drained
- 3 cups of cauliflower florets, chopped
- 3 cups of water
- 32 oz vegetable broth
- 2 stalks celery, chopped
- 1/4 tsp cayenne pepper
- 1/2 tsp ground ginger
- 2 tsp garlic, minced
- 1 tbsp ground turmeric
- 1 medium carrot, chopped
- 1 onion, diced
- 1 tbsp olive oil
- 7 oz noodles, drained
- 1/2 tsp pepper
- 1 tsp salt

Directions:

- Heat oil in a pan over medium heat.
- Add onion to the pan and sauté for 5 minutes.
- Add carrots and celery and sauté for 3 minutes.
- Add turmeric, garlic, ginger, and cayenne and sauté for a minute.
- Transfer pan mixture to the soup maker along with remaining ingredients and stir well.
- Seal the soup maker with its lid and cook on chunky mode.
- Serve and enjoy.

Nutritional Value (Amount per Serving):

- Calories 501
- Fat 6.6 g
- Carbohydrates 87.2 g
- Sugar 3.2 g
- Protein 31.5 g
- Cholesterol 10 mg

98-Classic Leek Potato Soup

Time: 40 minutes

Serve: 4

Ingredients:

- 1 lb potatoes, peeled and diced
- 2 leeks, sliced
- 3 garlic cloves, minced
- 2 tbsp butter
- 1/4 cup milk
- 4 cups of vegetable broth
- Pepper
- Salt

Directions:

- Melt butter in a pan over medium heat.
- Add garlic and leek to the pan and sauté for 5 minutes.
- Transfer sautéed leek and garlic to the soup maker along with remaining ingredients except for milk.

- Seal the soup maker with its lid and cook on blend mode for 25 minutes.
- Add milk and stir well.
- Season with salt and pepper.
- Serve and enjoy.

Nutritional Value (Amount per Serving):

- Calories 205
- Fat 7.7 g
- Carbohydrates 26.3 g
- Sugar 4.5 g
- Protein 8.1 g
- Cholesterol 17 mg

99-Sweet Corn Soup

Time: 35 minutes

Serve: 3

Ingredients:

- 1 ½ cups of corn kernels
- 3 cups of water
- 2 spring onion, chopped
- 4 beans, chopped
- ¼ cup carrots, chopped
- ¼ cup green peas
- 1 potato, peeled and chopped

Directions:

- Add all the ingredients to the soup maker.
- Cover soup maker with lid and cook on chunky mode.
- Season soup with salt and pepper.
- Serve warm and enjoy.

Nutritional Value (Amount per Serving):

- Calories 149
- Fat 1.1 g
- Carbohydrates 33 g
- Sugar 5.3 g
- Protein 5.9 g
- Cholesterol 0 mg

100-Broccoli Bean Soup

Time: 35 minutes

Serve: 4

Ingredients:

- 1 lb broccoli florets
- 14 oz can cannellini beans, drained
- 3 ½ cups of vegetable stock
- ¼ tsp red chili flakes
- 2 garlic cloves, minced
- 1 shallot, sliced
- 1 ½ tbsp olive oil
- Pepper
- Salt

Directions:

- Heat oil in a pan over medium heat.
- Add shallot to the pan and sauté for 4 minutes.
- Add garlic and sauté for a minute.

- Transfer sautéed shallot and garlic to the soup maker along with remaining ingredients.
- Seal the soup maker with its lid and cook on smooth mode.
- Season with salt and pepper.
- Serve and enjoy.

Nutritional Value (Amount per Serving):

- Calories 161
- Fat 6.8 g
- Carbohydrates 20.9 g
- Sugar 2.5 g
- Protein 7.7 g
- Cholesterol 0 mg

CONCLUSION:

In this soup maker cookbook, you will find a huge collection of healthy, delicious and nutritious soup recipes. This book will help people lose weight and lead a healthier lifestyle. All the recipes are made with a soup maker. A soup maker makes soup healthier and it prepares meals with essential nutrients such as vitamins, minerals, and proteins intact.

Thank you for downloading this book! I really do hope you found the recipes as delicious and mouth-watering as I did.

Happy Cooking!

Printed in Great Britain
by Amazon